SCRAMBLED
HOME EVENINGS

Other works by Joni Hilton

BOOKS

Braces, Gym Suits and Early Morning Seminary:
A Youthquake Survival Manual

Dating: No Guts, No Glory

As the Ward Turns

Around the Ward in 80 Days

Published by Running Press

Five Minute Miracles:
373 Quick Daily Projectsfor
You and Your Kids to Share

TAPES

Dating: No Guts, No Glory
(abridged from the book)

As the Ward Turns
(abridged from the book)

Caught in a Casserole

Around the Ward in 80 Days
(abridged from the book)

Scrambled Home Evenings
(abridged from the book)

Scrambled Home Evenings

A Novel by
Joni Hilton

Covenant Communications, Inc.
American Fork, Utah

For my mother, who took me to the doctor when I was seven to see why I wouldn't stop writing, and for my father, whose marvelous bedtime stories were the reason why.

Published by Covenant Communications, Inc.
American Fork, Utah

Copyright © 1994 by Joni Hilton
All rights reserved
Printed in the United States of America
First Printing: January 1994

00 99 98 97 96 95 94 93   10 9 8 7 6 5 4 3 2 1

Library of Congress Cataloging-in-Publication Data

Hilton, Joni, 1956–
    Scrambled home evenings : a novel / by Joni Hilton.
      p. cm.
    ISBN 1-55503-651-1
    1. Mormons—California—Fiction. 2. Family home
evenings (Mormon church)—Fiction. I. Title.
    PS3558.I4753S37   1994
    813'.54—dc20   93-42592
                          CIP

Special Thanks vi
An Interview with Edith Horvitz vii

1 Under the Big Top 1
2 The Name Game 9
3 Three's a Swarm 19
4 From the Frying Pan 27
5 Out of the Mouth of Babes' Mother 38
6 Through a Vale of Cheers 48
7 Loose Slips Sink Ships 59
8 A Bedtime Lullaby 65
9 Medals and Stars 70
10 The Mother of Inventions 77
11 Desperation and Inspiration 85
12 Mom-O'-War 91
13 The Gospel According to Edith 101
14 Video Mom 109
15 Dial-A-Disaster 117
16 Into the Fire 121
17 The Call of the Frugal Bugle 130
18 Have I Got a Job for You 137
19 Letting Edith's Light Shine 146
20 Scrambled Home Evenings 154
21 Off Like a Herd of Turtles 163
22 A Close Encounter with Erica 169
23 The History Lesson 176
24 The Secret Shared 183
25 Life with a Twist 187

SPECIAL THANKS

To Bob, the best husband, dad and malt-maker this side of the veil, for continuing to churn out wonderfully stealable material and wonderful high-calorie distractions.

And to our four children for their hilarious takes on life. I appreciate their unending support (some days more unending than others).

Thanks, also, to my dear friends, Karen Rogers, Cynthia Rhine, Christy Noll and Teru Miyashima, for living through—and sharing—so much comedy. Their real-life adventures have inspired many of Andy's fictional ones in *As the Ward Turns, Around the Ward in 80 Days,* and now *Scrambled Home Evenings.* (With friends like these, who needs an imagination?) Thanks for the years of roaring laughter, and for your loving tolerance of a writer buddy whose canoe's porch light is always one brick short of a picnic.

AN INTERVIEW
WITH EDITH HORVITZ

Q: Since you've been in *As the Ward Turns, Around the Ward in 80 Days,* and now *Scrambled Home Evenings,* I wonder if you might tell—

A: Obviously, you don't know what you're talking about. I wasn't just in those books. Those books are *starring* me. Have you read them?

Q: Uh, no, I just—

A: Well! How do you expect to understand anything I tell you, then?

Q: I just thought, perhaps, you could sort of summarize—

A: (snorts) Ha! Three books? Give me a break. I live a full life, honey. I can't just boil it down for you to conduct some quickie inner tube. Why haven't you read the first two books that set up this third one?

Q: Well, I was going to, but I've been waiting to borrow the ones that are circulating around my ward—

A: You *what?* Don't you realize this Hilton woman has four kids to put through college? Buy your own copies!

Q: Yes ma'am.

A: Wouldn't you like to read all about my fascinating inventions, my great ideas, my heroism, my charisma?

Q: Yes ma'am.

A: 'Course you would. And get some copies for your non-member friends, too. Wouldn't you like to show them what Mormon humor is all about?

Q: Yes ma'am.

A: All right, then. (pause) And sit up straight. You'll get round shoulders.

Q: Yes ma'am.

CHAPTER 1

UNDER THE BIG TOP

The thing they never tell you in Lamaze class is that before babies get teeth, they have pliers.

There you are, sitting with your husband, two pillows, and a belly that looks as if it should have its own zip code, and all you hear about is how to breathe and push. (It doesn't take many minutes of real labor to realize that a *man* thought this up. You even wonder if Lamaze could be French for masochism).

But the real surprise they never tell you about in those classes, is your next encounter in Pain's World, namely, nursing a child who thinks he's a land shark.

Multiply that by three, and you'll *almost* glimpse what happened when Brian and I (Brian included just for courtesy's sake; let's face it—*I* gave birth to those kids!) had triplets.

It all started, as you might remember, when we had an ultrasound and discovered that our posterity would now jump from a comfortable three to a staggering six, all in one swelled swoop. Brian banged his forehead on a stool as he fell into a faint, and I hyperventilated until a nurse made me breathe into a paper bag.

When the dust settled, we recognized a foundation of calm somewhere under all the shock. There was fear and panic, to be sure. But there was a peculiar thread of joy, too, lacing all our emotions together, and pushing little bursts of laughter to the surface. Three babies. *Three!*

The doctor began taking more measurements of me, and called in another doctor and two nurses to see the monitor. Brian and I stared at the screen with him, almost too overwhelmed to take it in at first. It was hard to breathe, and not just because three other people were crowding me for lung space. It was the crushing weight of responsibility. How do people *do* this? Could *we* do it? Brian's whole body was shaking, and I knew he was thinking what he could hock to afford three more children.

We looked at each other and grinned again. "I think we're delirious," Brian said. "This is not good news, right?"

I held my husband's shoulders. "It's wonderful news," I whispered with a lump in my throat.

"I couldn't do this with anyone else," Brian said, kissing my forehead and stroking my hair.

"You do and you're dead," I whispered.

"We are going to make it," he said, conviction in his voice. "I think we're just having a reaction to our hearts' expanding at triple speed."

I smiled. That was exactly how I was feeling. I loved those little ones already.

By now word had spread down the hall, and every technician and employee in the clinic was cheering and shouting congratulations.

Brian stared at the floor, smiling and wiping his tears. "This is incredible. We're actually going to have triplets."

The doctor patted Brian on the back. "Can I get you anything?"

"Oh, some strollers, cribs, high chairs, a bus—"

The doctor chuckled.

Brian kept mumbling. "Bicycles, braces, cars, scholarships . . . ."

As I laughed, the triplets seemed to somersault on the screen.

"Active babies," a nurse said.

"Nope, not acceptable," Brian said. "We ordered *passive* children, specifically. You'll have to exchange these."

I squeezed his hand. "And people wonder if God has a sense of humor."

We were immediately put in contact with wonderful support groups such as the Triplet Connection, and learned that less than 3,000 triplets are born in the United States each year. Of those, just a fraction are conceived spontaneously, without fertility drugs. These kids truly classified as ones in a million!

We decided to learn the sex of the babies through amniocentesis. Though I love a surprise, I felt my surprise quota was filled for this year quite nicely, thank you. By knowing the triplets' sex, we felt we could prepare at least somewhat. And, having had a girl and two boys already, I must confess I was hoping for three dainty, quiet, studious, pink-ribboned girls. Erica had been such an easy baby compared to her rambunctious brothers.

I held my breath as the doctor came into the examining room with my chart. He looked up, smiled at Brian and me, and said, "Three boys."

"No!" I gasped. Then, realizing I had slipped, and staring into the male faces of the only other people in the room, I said, "I mean, no kidding."

"Nice try," Brian smirked.

I sighed. Then I pleaded with the doctor. "Are they really boys? Are you sure?"

The doctor laughed. "All three. All boys."

I gulped and forced a smile as I looked at Brian.

He saw right through me. "This has been a hard day for you, hasn't it, honey?"

I moaned and leaned back on the examining table. "One girl and five boys. How can I be the mother of that many tube socks?"

Naturally the kids squealed with delight when we told them the news. Erica, our ten-year-old, literally leaped into the air and began dancing through the house. Grayson, eight, and Ryan, five, both declared the event "awesome," and gave each other a high five, as if they were personally responsible for this turn of events.

Friends and relatives reacted with elation (some of which was elation at not being in our same predicament), but everyone, it seemed, wanted to help supply us with furniture, clothes and other essentials. Through the whole pregnancy, members of our ward kept popping in with baby gear and meals for the weary mom (who, after the 20th week, was confined to bed). Needless to say, I was released as ward Relief Society president, and promptly plunked into a slot on the Activities Committee. I found this marvelously appropriate, since I was soon to be the ward expert on "activity."

Edith Horvitz, the homemaking director who had become a tycoon when she sold her "Stick 'Em Up Glue" to Nick's pharmaceutical company, had shared my initial dismay at our expecting all boys. "I was hoping you'd have one of each," she confided. I smiled at her arithmetic and tried not to look puzzled. (I still think it's a shame that the name Krazy Glue was already taken. It would have been so perfect in Edith's case.) I still marveled that the general public was hailing Edith as a genius. Not only didn't they take her insanity seriously; they cited it as a misdiagnosis of brilliance—almost definitive proof of her superior mental abilities. (They ought to travel with her, I thought to myself.) Edith was frequently written up in newspapers, asked to lecture around the world, and was constantly traveling to promote her invention.

Nick and Zan reacted in triplicate, arriving on our doorstep with a gorgeous three-seat stroller, each seat behind the next like train cars. "We know you won't need it for awhile," Zan said, "but we were too excited to wait."

Brian's mom sent three matching savings bonds in what we couldn't deny was the perfect size.

My mom and sisters reacted in perfect Butler fashion. Mom began her well-meaning warnings about triplet complications she was hoping wouldn't happen to me. Paula doubled up on her therapy sessions to learn how to cope with the trauma of being an aunt to triplets. And Natalie whistled and hooted for ten minutes over her good fortune at still being single.

After giving my family some deep thought, I decided that up in the spirit world, one boy had been getting ready to join our family when another peeked through the veil and gasped, "Wait—you can't go into that crazy family alone! I'm going with you." And another quickly piped up, "Me too."

Zan's parents, Olive and Irving Archer—America's Most Stoic Couple—said, "How lovely," and "What fine news." Their daughter, the Dutiful Wanda, murmured a formal "Congratulations."

These people will never have high blood pressure.

In no time, strangers were gawking at my middle (which was swelling like a bowl of bread dough on steroids) and saying, "Any day now, eh?" I became an expert teeth gritter.

Without belaboring (no pun intended) the colossal dimensions of my new figure, I will share just one example to illustrate the mammoth proportions we are talking here. You know those stores that have a little bell which dings as you walk in? Well, six months into this pregnancy, I went into such a store and the bell rang *twice*.

Two months before the triplets were born, the whole ward, husbands included, threw us a giant baby shower. I waddled up the walkway to the hostess' house, looking as if someone from Greenpeace should be following me in a boat, protecting me from getting speared. "If I faint," I whispered to Brian, "don't let anyone tattoo *Goodyear* on my side."

Our hostess opened the door and we walked into a home packed floor to ceiling with baby accessories. The outpouring of love was so overwhelming I cried (but then when I'm pregnant I cry over mouthwash commercials). Still, I had never seen so many baby accessories in my life. Edith built a seven-foot volcano out of diapers; and when the hostess announced that we should all go into the back yard for the eruption, Edith herself popped out of the top.

Brian, on whose balding head Edith had once glued a toupee, muttered, "Somebody's *gotta* find a way to donate her brain to science."

I laughed and hugged Edith, both of us stumbling over the Huggies avalanche. "I wanted to be practical," she said. "So I gave you this instead of my other idea."

"I hesitate to ask," Brian drawled, "but what was your other idea?"

"Three matching macaws!" Edith beamed. "Ones that don't talk yet, of course."

I glanced at Brian as we both remembered Angel, Edith's outspoken macaw with the, shall we say, colorful vocabulary. Even though Angel helped save the day when we were trying to capture Kirk and Stony in England, I wasn't ready to invite

another macaw—let alone three—into my home just yet. I
know the Church's stand on avoiding offensive language in
music, books and television; somehow I just know that's meant
to include parrots.

"Diapers will be much more useful," I agreed.

We had to remodel the house to make room for the new
babies, and the workmen finally left just as I was sure I couldn't
take any more enlarging—either of the house or of my body.

The triplets would have to be delivered cesarean. The week
before it was scheduled, while I was still bedridden, Nick and
Zan announced the fabulous news that they, too, were expecting. "However," Nick said, "we're going to take it one at a time."

Zan smiled at my gigantic middle, rising up under the bedspread like a levitation act. "We hope."

"A little cousin to grow up with!" I exclaimed. None of our
children had ever had any. Brian was an only child, Natalie had
never married, and Paula was on her third husband without
children. I had always prayed for cousins. "This is wonderful,"
I said. Dare I ask them to have a few more?

Finally the birthday morning came. Brian woke me up
shouting, "Delivery day!" like a UPS man. If only it could be
so simple, I thought.

Brian gave me one last blessing before we left for the hospital, and I felt a calm assurance that all would go smoothly.

The kids had begged us to let them name their new little
brothers, and we thought it would be a beautiful way to foster a close bond with them. Whenever anyone had asked if we
had picked names, Brian would say, "Eenie, Meenie, and
Miney, cause there won't be no mo'!"

But in fact, we had let the children select their favorite
names during a family home evening, and we had all agreed
to keep it a surprise. Erica had picked Michael, Grayson had
picked Don, and Ryan had picked Godfrey.

At last, I thought to myself as I was wheeled into the hospital elevator, the waiting is finally over. As they strapped
me onto the gurney and wheeled me to the operating room,
Brian squeezed my hand. "I love you," he whispered.

Through a happy lump in my throat I squeaked, "Me too."

"You scared?" he asked. I'd never had a C-section before. I shook my head. "Just wonderfully happy."

And then, as he does every time we have a baby, Brian leaned down to my ear and said, "Hang in there. Just think, more little kiddos to take to Disneyland." The thought had helped me through labor when I'd had Erica; so just before our children are born, Brian always suggests this carefree image of our family laughing together at Disneyland.

I could picture it perfectly—the manicured flower beds, the bright balloons, the whirling rides. In my mind's eye, I saw our triplets posing with Mickey, Donald, and Goofy—

"BRIAN, WAIT!" I shrieked, trying to sit up. "We can't do this!"

"Andy, get a grip," Brian said, trying to lie me back down again. "I don't think we have a whole lot of choice here—"

"I mean, Michael and Don and Godfrey! Don't you get it?"

"Get what?"

"The kids! They've tricked us! They're trying to get us to name the kids after Mickey, Donald and Goofy!"

"What!" Brian pushed me back down again, and a nurse laid a calming hand on my shoulder.

I kept climbing up Brian's arm just the same. "It's collusion!" I yelled. "The kids are trying to dupe us!"

"Which kids—the first three or the new three?" Beads of sweat were breaking out on Brian's forehead as he tried to control his hysterical wife.

"Erica, Grayson and Ryan!" I shouted. "They picked those names so they can twist them into cartoon characters!"

We pushed through some swinging doors and Brian tried to swallow and take in the gravity of the upcoming operation. "Look, let's just have the babies and talk about names later, okay?"

"You'd better believe we will!" I shouted. "And when I get my hands on those three—"

Our doctor was waiting inside for us, and stared in disbelief at my furious threat, which hung in the air like the world's first case of prepartum blues.

Immediately the nurse began whispering to him, tattling about my emotional state.

Dr. Sanders stepped solemnly to my side, as if I were an organ donor on life support. "Mrs. Taylor," he said, no doubt drawing upon a psychiatry class he took twenty years ago, "are you feeling all right?"

"She's fine," Brian said, embarrassed to the hilt.

"I need Mrs. Taylor to answer," Dr. Sanders said.

"Oh, like this is some mental test!" I snapped. "You have no idea how close we came to lifetime humiliation for our children!"

"I think we've guaranteed it for the dad," Brian deadpanned, glancing at me to button it *now*.

"They nearly got away with it!" I shouted back at Brian. "Do you realize what would have happened if I had filled out that name form before I caught on?"

Brian was shrugging and smiling, chuckling softly to the anesthesiologist. One of his hands was mechanically—and uselessly—patting my arm.

"Mickey, Donald, and Goofy—over my fat body!" I roared.

"It's hormones," I heard Brian whisper for the millionth time during this pregnancy.

"It is *not!*" I growled. "It is a near calamity that I discovered in the nick of time! Literally."

Brian leaned close to my face now, looking ready to anesthetize me with his bare hands, and said with forced composure, "Andy, we will discuss names *later.*"

I stared into his desperate eyes, which were watering with embarrassment, and laughed. Rarely have I heard Brian issue a command with such clarity and finality. This is one guy who takes very seriously the Church's directive to treat a wife as an equal and involve her in all decisions. To see Brian bossing me—in public, yet—was a real hoot.

While I was still cracking up, Brian nodded to Dr. Sanders and something cool and sleepy began flowing into my I.V. tube. Slowly the funny image of Brian barking orders at me faded into fuzzy amusement, and the last thing I heard was Brian's ludicrous comment that the entire pregnancy had been a roller coaster ride on a hormone loop-de-loop. I made a mental note to sock him one later, and fell asleep.

CHAPTER 2

THE NAME GAME

The next thing I knew, Brian was kissing me and whispering, "Congratulations, Mommy. We have three beautiful little boys."

I felt myself coming out of the anesthesia, having forgotten all about my plan to sock Brian. There he was, the darling man I married, holding a tiny little bundle in his arms. Two nurses were on my other side, each holding matching blue blankets wrapped around red-faced, wrinkled, precious babies that were mewing like newborn kittens.

"Oh!" I said, looking from one precious face to the next. "They're so tiny!" All our others had tipped the nine-pound mark, and these looked only half as big.

"They're good-sized for triplets," one nurse said. "All healthy."

"They're identical," the other nurse said. "A perfect little set of three."

I cried as one of the nurses handed me two of the little boys. "Little sweethearts," I whispered. "I love you."

Brian rested the third boy on my chest and took a picture. "You feeling okay?" He kissed my cheek.

"Yes! I don't feel a thing," I said, thinking I'd never had such an easy delivery. The nurses exchanged knowing glances, and it wasn't long before the anesthetic wore off and I discovered that "easy" is not a word many women would use to describe a C-section.

Still, my first few minutes with the triplets were pure heaven. I could literally feel my capacity to love growing threefold, and the spiritual joy that enveloped us was truly indescribable.

After I was situated in my hospital room, Brian brought Erica, Grayson and Ryan (a.k.a. The Culprits) in. After hello kisses and hugs, I got right down to business. "So. You guys thought you had us fooled, didn't you?"

"Fooled about what?" Erica said.

"The names," I sneered. "Mickey, Donald, and Goofy."

Erica grinned. "Oh, that."

"Dang!" Grayson said. "They found out!"

Ryan looked like he'd been caught robbing a bank.

"You are no longer in charge of naming the triplets," Brian said.

Ryan gulped. "It was their idea," he said, starting to cry.

I held my arms out and he fell onto my stomach. "Oof!" Not a good plan. Ryan scooted onto the edge of the bed and I held him. "We know, Honey. It's okay."

Grayson sputtered. "How do you know it was our idea? You'll believe anything Ryan says!"

"Grayson," I said, "do you expect me to believe that a five-year-old came up with the name Godfrey?"

Grayson chewed his cheek, trying to think of a plausible explanation.

"A name is a very special thing—" Brian began.

"Hey, I know what we can name them!" Grayson interrupted, not a shred of repentance in his voice. "Leonardo, Raphael, and Michelangelo—the artists!" Then he grinned as if he had surprised us with his vast cultural expertise.

"We are not naming them after Ninja Turtles," Brian said. "Besides, there are only three babies."

I stared at Brian. "Oh, you'd consider it if they had been quadruplets?"

"Okay," Erica said, joining in Grayson's mischief, "How about Alvin, Theodore, and Simon?"

"No—Huey, Duey, and Luey!" Grayson evidently thought this was a brainstorming session.

"Your father and I will choose the names," I said, my eyes narrowing into slits at the thought of our sons saddled with the monikers of ducks and chipmunks.

Just then a nurse brought me a wheelchair, so we could all go look at the triplets in the nursery. As we stared at our babies in their little isolettes, a new father stepped up to the window beside Brian and said, "That little girl with the dark hair is mine."

Brian made approving sounds and the fellow said, "Hey— I just doubled the number of kids I have!"

Brian smiled. "Me too."

"Did you have a boy or a girl?" the man asked.

"Three boys."

The young father's eyes shot open. "Whoa! Triplets? Let's see, then . . ." he began counting on his fingers.

"It's six," Grayson said. Then brightly to his withering father, "Wow, we have so many kids now, people have to count us on their fingers!"

Two nurses rolled our triplets up to the windows, and suddenly a crowd began to form. Other new parents, their relatives and five or six hospital workers were all crowding to see our babies and congratulate us. I beamed with pride as our little wonders elicited so much excitement.

"What are their names?" someone asked.

"Well," Brian said, tossing a warning glance at the children, "we haven't decided, yet. Anybody have any ideas?"

Suddenly the hall seemed filled with a hundred voices, everyone eager to share their favorites. Brian grinned at me and I shrugged; this was certainly a better technique than Plan A had been.

After visits from our mothers, some friends, the new Relief Society president and my visiting teachers, we sent the kids home with their grandmothers. Finally, Brian and I were alone with the triplets in our hospital room.

"You want to talk about names?" Brian asked hesitantly, remembering the intensity of my earlier feelings on the subject.

I laughed. "I'm sorry I was so upset."

Brian shrugged as if he handled psychotics for a living. "No-o-o problem."

I stared into the faces of our little guys, looking for a clue.

"I think I want their names to be different from each other," I said.

"Yes, I think identical triplets will be confusing enough already," Brian said.

At that moment, some nurses came in to check my stitches, give me a pill, and take my blood pressure. Each one stopped to coo and fuss over the triplets, rave about how gorgeous they were, and tell us what a great blessing this was. I stared at the nurses' name tags, then said, "Brian—look. Those would be perfect names!"

He looked at me as if I were nuts. These were *women* I was pointing to.

"I mean their last names," I said. "Austin, Bennett, and Cameron."

Brian whispered the names over and over to himself, thinking about each one as the nurses giggled and went about their work.

"I like those," he said. "But which one for which boy?"

I laughed. "Hey—A, B, and C." And thus it was—names we liked, with a sense of "famous threesomes" for the older kids.

The next day Edith Horvitz came by, bumping into Brian in the hallway. "Sister Horvitz—come and see the babies we had," Brian said, escorting her to the nursery window.

"Whaddaya mean 'we'?" she snapped. "Unless you've ever passed a small condominium—all corners—I'd say you didn't have much to do with it."

"Andy would appreciate your sentiments," Brian said. Then he pointed to our boys. "There's Austin, Bennett, and that's Cameron by the rocking chair."

Edith tapped on the window and pressed her maroon-lipsticked face against the glass. "It's Auntie Edith!" she sang. "Hey, look at those guys—they've got my hair!"

Sure enough, Edith's balding frizz was a good match for the peach fuzz on our triplets. Brian was about to say, "Mine, too," but he didn't want to invite another toupee-and-glue attack.

Then she came into my room and handed me a tiny package to open. "Gotta start those kids off right, listening to good music," she said.

I stared as I opened the gift, not believing my eyes.

"Cut myself an album," Edith said, rocking proudly on her heels.

Sure enough, it was a cassette tape of Edith singing "Hits of the '60s" with the London Philharmonic Orchestra. Now that Edith was a multimillionaire, she figured she'd hire the best, and we were among the fortunate first to receive a copy.

"I just don't know what to say," I murmured.

"You and the queen both," Edith said. "I gave her a buzz while I was over there."

She gave the queen of England a buzz?

Edith went on. "I figured since she'd had us to lunch and gave me that teapot, I ought to drop in. Long as I was in town."

Our jaws dropped open.

"Her secretary said she was under the weather," Edith said. Then she rolled her eyes as if that were the most obvious thing she'd ever heard. "I mean, aren't we all?" Edith gestured toward the ceiling and the sky of weather that lay beyond. "So I popped a tape in the mail to her."

"And she called you?" Brian was dumbfounded.

"Nah. I called her before I left." Edith poured herself a glass of water with my bedside pitcher. "She came to the phone and said she had gotten the tape, and just didn't know what to say. How 'bout that? I left her speechless."

We knew how she felt.

Edith gave us a wry grin, the picture of smug delight. "I hired me a publicist, y'know. I figure that's the only way to get any air time."

"Air time?" Brian and I were growing more amazed by the minute.

"Sure. I want my songs on every radio station in the country." This woman and Ross Perot should compare advertising accounts.

I remembered Edith's singing on our trip to Europe and tried to imagine the sort of station that would play it. Was there a station KNUT? What would be their slogan—"All Nuts, All The Time"?

"Well, gotta go," Edith said, downing the last of my water.

"Gotta get over to IHOP before six for the Early Bird Special."

"Thank you for the tape," Brian and I called after her as she headed off to buy liver and lima beans for $4.99 at the local House of Pancakes.

I soon discovered that while I was in the hospital, Brian had taken over my bedtime story duties, and changed my "Polly the Penguin" series into "Vinnie the Vulture" tales. But my chagrin at being so rapidly replaced was quickly forgotten in the task of devising ways to tell the boys apart. Brian's mom suggested we paint different colors of nail polish on their toenails, but we found that babies' nails are so soft that the polish doesn't stay on for long. Then my mom suggested dressing each boy in one color of clothing, but that became utterly impractical when we tried to keep up with the laundry and sorting.

The triplets didn't have enough hair to style in various distinguishing ways, nor did even one of them have a stray mole or cowlick to help us.

Not surprisingly, Edith Horvitz offered to glue tiny name tags on them. "Uh . . ." I said, stalling for a gracious excuse.

Then Edith slapped herself on the forehead. "Why didn't I think of this?" she said. "Tattoos!"

Brian and I just smiled (actually Brian made a low, rumbling noise like a volcano getting ready to erupt), and as politely as I could, I said, "I don't think so, Edith."

And then, during a family home evening, we got them mixed up. Erica had strung an old sheet across a string, cut a low window in it, and was planning to use the triplets in their baby seats as puppets. Carefully she arranged them behind the sheet. But with her brothers as assistants, the triplets got scooted out of order.

We finally had to go to the police station and compare footprints (which is tricky already, since identical babies' footprints are very much alike). The woman helping us was even more confused than we were, and thought Bennett—the only one we were sure about—was one of the others. She even put a gentle hand on my shoulder and said, "Well, what does it really matter?"

"It matters!" I gasped. At last her supervisor helped us

sort things out, and from then on we kept different colored, stretchy ponytail bands on their wrists.

Their blessing day was unforgettable. Brian gave each boy such personal and distinct blessings and promises that I felt their personalities and special gifts were unfolding before me. I could even discern needs that I, as a mother, would need to know. It's breathtaking to see the priesthood in action. And, naturally, it took up a good portion of fast and testimony meeting.

After the meeting, Monica, my former education counselor, was hugging me as Brian came and stood beside us. "Did I get everything in?" he asked, as though I had dictated a list of traits for him to remember. (Okay, okay. So I had mentioned one or two things).

"Now you know why the blessing duties fall to the men," Monica chuckled. "Because if mothers blessed the babies, we'd just keep going on and on and on!"

Brian nodded and I poked him. I could still remember our blessing discussion when Erica had been born. Like the fairies in "Sleeping Beauty," we had stood over her bassinet, sharing our hopes and dreams for her future. Somehow I had the mistaken notion that it would be fun to know what Brian would bless *me* with, if my life were just beginning. (Bear in mind that I had just been rear-ended at a stoplight by a Dodge Ram.)

"I would bless you with no car wrecks," Brian smiled.

I lowered my eyebrows. "Well, I would bless *you* with the realization that none of them were my fault."

"Then I'd bless you with the knowledge that insurance doesn't care."

"Then I'd bless you with generosity, so you'd buy the right kind of insurance in the first place" We were nose to nose now, and had we been actual fairies, we'd have been whacking each other with our wands.

"I'm sorry I asked," I finally hissed.

"Now you know why I didn't," Brian replied. Thereafter I gave a little less input on the babies' blessings.

The next few months were the most exhausting I have ever known. This was baptism by fire—or at least oatmeal—into multiple parenting. The triplets ate so ravenously that I wondered if maybe they *were* land sharks. Maybe that's why there were three—because they weren't entirely human and this was, in fact, a litter.

They were such vigorous nursers—nothing like the first three kids—that I could only assume they were trying to get their weight up. We supplemented my nursing with bottles of formula, and Brian timed Bennett (our number one gobbler) at emptying eight ounces in as many seconds. Their effect on my body was staggering.

Finally, I put my embarrassment aside and went to a dermatologist to see if the bruising would be permanent.

The doctor stared at my chest as if examining a strange malfunction in the buttons of a VCR. Then he insisted I disrobe completely to see if I bruised easily elsewhere on my body. I cringed. Now that I was a professional milking machine, I had neglected to shave my legs that morning, or to rub lotion over my scaly white skin. Even my toes were in need of fresh polish.

"If you don't make this quick," I said as he came back into the room, "I'll break out in hives and we'll never know if I'm bruised or not."

The doctor squinted as he scanned every inch of my body. "I don't see any unusual bruises," he said.

"How about a bruised ego?" I asked as I sat up and drew the paper smock around me.

"Let's follow this after you stop nursing, and keep an eye on it," he smiled. "Maybe it's just idiopathic."

What does that mean—the result of idiocy? There was no way I was going to ask him for a definition and thus substantiate the diagnosis!

Brian and I were in bed before I finally had time to tell him about the doctor visit. "He said it was because I'm an idiot," I said, coming to the end of my adventure. Brian didn't even flinch, but seemed to take the news in stride. I swatted him with a pillow. "You could have acted a least a *little* surprised."

"Surprised by what?" Brian had nodded off during my story.

"By my being an idiot."

Brian blinked and tried to wake up. "Why should that surprise me?"

Now I threw myself onto him, trying to pound him as he hung onto my wrists and protested. "Hey—what is this—I was sound asleep, and suddenly there's a crazy woman beating her fists on my chest!"

"Because you said I was an idiot!" I laughed, trying to look tough and dig my elbows into his sides.

"I did not!" Brian held my arms firmly to each side. "*You* said you were an idiot. I merely agreed."

"How can you be such a—a—" my mind was blowing fuses faster than firecrackers, and I couldn't think of a good comeback.

"Hey, you're the one who let some doctor see you completely naked today—and *paid* him for it!"

I growled into his face. "*I was humiliated!*"

Brian chuckled. "Your own fault."

"Oh, what was I supposed to do—refuse? I felt completely . . . violated."

"Violated by a standard medical exam." Brian smiled and shook his head. "You ought to go through the kind of physicals men have to have." He pulled me into an embrace, and I finally let go of the fury and sank, exhausted, into his arms.

"How can you let a little exam like that embarrass you, when you've had six children?" Brian asked.

I sighed. "Because those times . . . my legs were always shaved."

Brian laughed. "That's what this is about—that you didn't shave your legs? Sheesh! I'm going to sleep. Goodnight." Brian turned over and pulled the blankets over his shoulders.

I realized how foolish I was being and snuggled up to his back, pressing up against him like we were two spoons. I felt better, now that Brian had let me know how silly I was being.

"Yeow!" Brian screeched, pulling his legs away. "That leg stubble is really bristly!" He sat up and turned the light on. "I think I could be bleeding," he said, pretending to examine his own legs for cuts.

"You are the most obnoxious man I know," I said, as Brian leaned into my face and grinned.

"It's on purpose," he whispered.

No kidding.

Brian went on in smug delight. "I'm in a class by myself, aren't I?"

I fumed. "You keep this up and you'll soon be in a *bed* by yourself."

Brian rubbed his legs again. "That might be safer . . ."

"You know what I think I'll do?" I said, lying back on my pillow and drumming my fingers on my stomach. "I think I'll stop shaving my legs altogether. Just like in Europe. No—as a tribute to the newly democratic countries of Russia." (This always infuriates my history professor husband, who loves to correct those who think that Russia—one republic—is the catchall name for the entire bunch.)

Brian sneered and climbed back into bed. "I know you're saying Russia on purpose."

Victory. I enjoyed a grand sigh, then said, "I'm in a class by myself, aren't I?"

CHAPTER 3

THREE'S A SWARM

My vision had changed after this pregnancy. So, despite my uncomfortable experience with the dermatologist, I soon found myself in the examining room of an ophthalmologist, who—I felt certain—would not need me to disrobe based on my inability to read an eye chart. But just in case, I picked a female doctor.

She scooted up close on her rolling stool, and leaned into my face with a bright light.

"For being so nearsighted, your eyes are in terrific shape," she said. "I don't see any stretch marks on your retina."

Finally—somewhere on my body that doesn't have stretch marks! Ah . . . life's little celebrations.

As I wheeled the triplets out with my new prescription, people in the waiting room stopped me with the standard reactions we've come to expect: "You sure have your hands full," "I'll bet you'll quit now," and "I'm just glad they're not mine!" (to which I sometimes think, "So are they.") Another oft-heard comment is, "What a blessing," which always buoys me up after a morning of feeding and changing, feeding and changing.

I realized that I now tack on an extra 45 minutes anytime I go anywhere, to allow for crowd commentary. Just buckling and unbuckling three infants into three car seats adds ten minutes. And making sure I have enough diapers and bottles on hand feels like I'm packing for a trip.

A trip—what is that? Would I ever have a weekend getaway with Brian again? We love our family vacations with the kids, but it would be so romantic to stroll along a secluded beach, hand in hand with him, and not have to constantly whip my head around to look for children, or to smear sunscreen over another little scrunched-up face, or to shell out money for another soft drink, or to hunt for a missing sandal.

On the other hand . . . I realized that despite the exhaustion and the endless demands, I was blissfully happy and felt blessed beyond my wildest dreams. This was the toughest job on the planet, but the most rewarding one, too. I can't describe for a mother who has never had multiples, how amazing it feels to hold three babies, look into their little faces—all at the same stage of wonder—and see a triple measure of love coming back to you. As I often tell the children when they tease me for crying easily, sometimes you're just so full of the Spirit that your body can't hold it all, and it leaks out your eyes.

Erica, Grayson, and Ryan enjoyed that same glow of abundant love, too—at first. They became wildly popular at school and couldn't wait to show off their new brothers to all their sudden friends. Grayson even enjoyed standing behind me while I played pat-a-cake with the babies, cupping his hands over his mouth and making a beat box rhythm (until I caught on, anyway).

Then, after the honeymoon, the first year unrolled into a seemingly endless assembly line of diapers and laundry. When we weren't feeding the babies, we were changing them. And our evenings became laundry home evenings every night, sorting and folding.

Despite tremendous help from the Relief Society sisters— many staying hours to help rock, bathe and feed the babies— the first year was an exhausting blur. As I fell into bed with Brian one night, both of us silently praying for an hour of rest, I said, "I honestly wonder if I'll remember anything from this period of time, except their faces and bottoms."

I was glad I didn't have triplets first, or I might have thought this exhausting lifestyle was the normal pattern of parenting (and I would be writing this on paper towels from the mental hospital). But gratefully, I remembered the infancies of Erica, Grayson, and Ryan, and I knew that this sleepless, zombie period wouldn't last forever.

Our older kids had no such frame of reference, however, and thus became celebrities by day, grumblers by night. Brian and I watched them progress through the stages of triplet adjustment as if it were the stages of grief.

First there was shock. Ryan was aghast at the hundreds of diapers we zoomed through each month. Grayson was mortified by how much three babies could actually spit up. And Erica was completely unable to believe that the triplets cried so much in the night. "You must be doing something wrong," she sneered one morning, as if Brian and I were secretly withholding the tricks one uses to lull a baby to sleep.

Then there was denial. Ryan would play happily in the same noisy room with his three hungry brothers, engrossed in his Legos and oblivious to their cries. Erica, who had cried with joy when she first held them, was now "totally busy" with homework whenever I needed her. And Grayson, too, would ignore them, bounding up the stairs to his room at the first hint of a whimper (which could mean a request from me for some help). Instead, he would disappear into a fantasy world of Mighty Morphine Power Rangers.

"That's *morphin'*," he corrected me one day when I had called them mighty morphine. "Morph means to change," he said, thankfully supplying me with my recommended daily allowance of Latin. "The Green Ranger transforms into the green Dragon Zord." Well, obviously a wet diaper is going to have to go a long way to compete with a distraction like that.

"Fine," I said one day, feeling exactly like the Little Red Hen whom no one would help, "when these triplets turn out fantastic, *I'm* taking all the credit myself!"

"Okay by me," Grayson said, stuffing a handful of potato chips into his mouth. Somehow the Little Red Hen just doesn't work as a baby-sitting motivator.

The next stage was anger. When a woman at the supermarket exclaimed, "Triplets—how fun!" a sullen Ryan pouted, "They're not as much fun as you think." And Grayson, after fruitless efforts to tune out the constant noise level, clamped his hands over his ears and screamed, "QUIET!" as if the triplets would then hush themselves, winking at one another.

Erica, whose stream of new friends clamored for her time until the novelty faded, blamed the triplets for the dip in her popularity. "Look at this place!" she complained. "It's so full of baby junk you can't move. How can I invite anybody over?"

I had to admit that if someone were to label the style and decor of our house just then, it would be "Early Childhood Education."

We were still waiting for the older children to advance to the acceptance stage, but that loomed far in the distance.

Trying to shift the focus to Erica, Grayson and Ryan, I devised three family home evenings, each of which would usher in a week starring one of them. The first lesson was all about Erica. We looked at her scrapbooks, watched a video of her ballet recital, showered her with compliments and fixed her favorite dessert. That week we all made her bed, did her chores, and lavished her with attention.

Little did I know how spoiled a person can become after a week of unbridled adulation. When the next Monday rolled around, I discovered that we had created a monster. Erica whined about making her bed, groused about ironing her own blouse, and even rolled her eyes at having to pour her own milk.

"Her majesty is sitting in the carriage, awaiting her footman," I said to Brian as Erica slammed the front door and plopped down in the back seat of the car, waiting to be driven to school.

Brian grinned. "It's such a beautiful day," he said, the wheels turning. "Seems a shame to spend it in a car. Let's let her walk to school."

Thus, Erica came home that day crying that her feet were blistered (this is a fifteen-minute walk) and accusing us of being the meanest parents in the world. She felt we had absolutely set her up, just to yank all our love and caring out from under her.

I cringed, sorry I had ever conjured up such a backfire. I dreaded that night's lesson on Grayson, but there was no backing out. He had been counting the days until it was *his* turn to O.D. on all this pampering.

For the first time ever, he flew through his dinner, washed

the dishes in record speed, then sat expectantly in the living room, awaiting his coronation with a big smile. Earlier, he had even morphed a diaper.

I swallowed and began. Out came the scrapbook. Out came the video of his last baseball game. Out came the compliments. Out came the favorite dessert. Everything was exactly as we had done for Erica.

"This isn't fair!" Grayson frowned. "You had more pictures of Erica."

"Erica is older," I said, having meticulously kept just as careful a scrapbook for each child, in my obviously futile attempt to avoid this very problem.

"And I looked terrible playing baseball. I hit a foul."

"I thought it was a good, strong hit," I said, thinking, hey— at least you hit it.

"And those compliments aren't as good as the ones you gave Erica," he whined.

"You want us to tell you what a fine young lady you are?" Brian asked.

"No!" Grayson scowled.

"Is the cake acceptable, Your Highness?" I asked him.

"You didn't let me pick which piece I wanted."

"Grayson," I sighed. "It's a round cake. All the pieces are identical."

"Hey—triplet cake!" Erica said.

"See?" Grayson pounced on her comment. "This isn't my night. Even the cake is about the triplets!"

"I quit," Brian said, swinging a dish cloth over its hook.

"You can't quit before *my* night!" Ryan gasped.

I held my breath. Two down and one to go.

For Ryan's family home evening, we dragged out an even more meager collection of photos and even less distinguished video (Ryan wiggling his tongue and getting too close to the lens). The compliments were sounding a little too worn and familiar, and even the dessert, my killer brownies, got bumped off the number one spot on Ryan's list of favorites.

"I thought you loved brownies," I said. "When did you change your mind?"

"Oh . . ." Ryan said, dangling his feet off the stool at the breakfast bar, "about an hour ago."

Timing is everything. Now his favorite dessert was strawberry shortcake—*fresh* strawberry shortcake—and this was November.

"And now we have to be his slaves for a week," Brian said as we got into bed that night. "I wonder if he'll be like Grayson." Grayson had refined the sultan's double hand clap to summon his servants, and had been milking this thing for a solid week.

"Do you realize," I muttered, "that if we had one of those lamps that come on when you clap, our house would have looked like a strobe display this week?"

But Ryan had his own style. He chose to go limp when it was time to get dressed, until we bodily threaded his arms through his sleeves as if he were a baby. He spent the week feigning exhaustion and utter incompetence.

My grand scheme to convince each child of his or her special worth had only made self-centered egomaniacs out of them. When Ryan's week ended, Brian and I made a solemn pact: No more family home evenings that could backfire. We hoped.

"At least I burned a few more calories this month," I said, trying to look on the bright side and recalling the extra work it had been, as Brian and I got ready for bed. Maybe now I could segue from my fat-fat pants to my fat pants.

Brian stepped into the shower while I brushed my teeth. I listened as the pipes squealed and shook. We had put a call in to our plumber, Anders Johansson, a Church member from Minnesota who had moved into the ward last year, but he hadn't called back in three days. Maybe I'd have to find someone else.

"I think you're losing a lot of weight," Brian called over the noise, trying to encourage me.

It was seven months after the triplets' birth and I was still carrying far too many pounds to feel good about it. I was nursing, so a strict diet was out of the question. It was hard to fight the discouragement (and the truffles by the sportswear at

Nordstrom's). If I weren't taking the triplets with me everywhere I went, I felt sure someone would ask me when I was due.

"I'd like to lose about ten pounds," Brian said as he stepped out of the shower and began drying off his back.

"Ha!" I scoffed, at a man who couldn't "pinch an inch" if you paid him. Then, turning to stare at his perfectly flat stomach—and his ludicrous desire to lose weight—I said, "Look at you! You are nothing!"

Brian froze, holding his towel in midair behind his neck.

Suddenly I broke up laughing and fell to the floor, realizing what I had just said to a naked man. I had meant it as a real compliment, but Brian's expression told me I had most definitely miscommunicated.

"I can't believe I said that," I roared, rolling myself up in a little rug.

"I *am* some*buddy*," Brian said, pointing an accusing finger at me and using his best Jesse Jackson accent. Okay, so he was being a good sport. But it was too late. That first split second of shock on his face was priceless—worth a ten-minute laugh, easy. Brian watched me giggle until tears were streaming down my cheeks. He stared at his wife, curled up in a ball on the floor, then sighed, "And me without a camera."

After I had run out my rope he asked, "Are you planning to spend the night rolled up in a bath mat?"

I pulled myself to my feet, worn out and watery-eyed. Little chuckles kept erupting as I finished getting ready for bed. "That didn't come out how I wanted it to," I said at last, putting my arms around Brian and trying to make up.

"I gathered."

"I meant that you're so slim," I said, nuzzling him. "In college, that's what we'd say to a skinny girl who thought she was fat. It means that your waist is so tiny, it's like nothing."

Brian glanced at me out of the corner of his eye. "And this was considered a compliment."

I nodded vigorously. "Yeah!"

Now he shook his head. "Women."

"So do you think the triplets will sleep through the night?" I asked, trying to change the subject.

Brian just stared at me. "How could I possibly know that?"

I sputtered. "Well, of course you don't *know,* but maybe you could speculate. It's just a point of conversation."

Brian just stared at me. "How could I possibly guess? What kind of crazy question is that?"

"I see. So when a man says, 'You think the Lakers are gonna beat Boston?' you tell him you couldn't possibly know, and what a ridiculous question that is."

"Of course not," Brian said. "I tell him what I think."

"But it's speculation because nobody knows. You guys are just talking sports and guessing about the game."

"That's different," Brian said.

"No it's not," I argued. "I'm talking triplets and guessing about tonight."

Brian sighed. "Okay, I think two of them will sleep but one of them will blow it and get traded to St. Louis."

"Thank you," I said. Men just don't know how to have conversations.

CHAPTER 4

FROM THE FRYING PAN . . .

As it turned out, the triplets did sleep through the night, for the first time ever. (And it was the last time for several months afterwards, but I still wrote it in their baby books). "Some sportscaster you turned out to be," I said to Brian. But at least he got to enjoy a night's rest. As for me, I kept waking up and listening for them; so by morning, I was as exhausted as ever.

The boys had been fussy about nursing all that week, arching their backs and screaming as though I had suddenly substituted lemon juice on them. By noon when they still wouldn't nurse, I called my obstetrician, Dr. Sanders. The receptionist said he was delivering a baby, but she'd have him call me as soon as possible.

Thankfully, Brian's teaching schedule allowed him to be home during the late afternoons so that he could help the older three with their homework before heading off again to teach evening classes. Today he got home in time to take Grayson to his baseball game.

Just as Grayson was getting his uniform on, the phone rang. I was changing Austin, so Brian answered the call. "It's Sanders," he said, trading me a phone for a baby so that he could help Grayson find all his baseball paraphernalia.

Thank heavens. "I'm so glad you called back," I said into the receiver. "I'm having such a problem. This started on Monday and I don't even know if anything's coming out. Maybe that's why they scream so much. Maybe everything's just stopped up."

"Could be," Dr. Sanders said.

"Or maybe it's changed to soda water," I joked. "Who knows?"

"Well, let's have a look."

"Can you still squeeze me in today?"

"I can be there in ten minutes."

"Oh my heavens—this must be serious if you're coming to the house!"

"How else can I check your faucets?" he asked.

How crude, I thought. "You mean you want to check my *breasts,*" I corrected. I wasn't going to have them referred to as faucets, even if that's the way my life was going of late.

There was complete silence on the other end. Undoubtedly I had embarrassed Dr. Sanders, but I felt fully justified in speaking up.

"Sister Taylor, I think perhaps you'd better get another plumber," he said at last. Then he hung up.

I stood there, dazed. Then suddenly it hit me. I had not been talking to Dr. Sanders at all, but to Anders Johansson, the plumber!

Brian came around the corner and put Austin down on a rug to play. "So is he coming over to look at the pipes?"

Well, there was nothing to do now but scream, so that is exactly what I did, until Brian sat me down on a chair and almost had to shake me to get me to stop. "What is the matter with you?" he shouted.

"We have to move," I wailed. "I know I've said this before, but this time I'm serious. We have to move, Brian. I'm calling a realtor right now and listing the house."

"What are you talking about—just because we have to replace some *pipes?*"

I tried to swallow but my mouth was completely dry. "I'm running away. You and the kids can come with me if you like. But either way, I'm going to Brazil or someplace."

Brian looked into my pale, panicky face as a smile crept slowly across his. "Let me guess. You've embarrassed yourself again, haven't you?"

I slapped him on the chest with both hands. "You don't know that!" I snarled.

Brian laughed. "Okay, let's hear it."

I blinked a mile a minute, trying to gather the pieces together and figure out how the conversation could go on and on like it did, without Brother Johansson realizing that I thought he was my doctor. Surely it had been obvious. What was the matter with him? And why on earth had Brian told me it was Dr. Sanders in the first place?

"This is all your fault!" I said, furious and fighting the tears.

"Why am I not surprised?" Brian smirked. "How is it my fault this time?"

"I spilled my whole, personal medical problem out to Anders Johansson!" I shouted. "I told him to look at my breasts!! Aaugh!"

Brian squinted at me. "Why on earth would you do that?"

"Because you said it was Sanders!"

"I said, 'It's Anders.' You don't listen."

"You don't enunciate! You ran that whole sentence together so it came out 'It's Sanders.'"

Brian was laughing now. "You actually asked him—"

"No!" I interrupted. "You are not going to get one speck of pleasure out of this, Brian Taylor. I want you to call Brother Johansson back this very minute and explain what happened and how this was all your fault."

He was chuckling as Grayson bounded down the stairs and out the front door. "I can't," Brian said. "I have to take Grayson to his game. He's waiting."

"Well, he can just wait!" I said, feeling myself getting more hysterical by the minute. "This is critical!"

"So is this game," Brian said. "And Grayson needs me to be there."

"Fine," I growled through my teeth. "You stay here and feed three hungry triplets and *I'll* sit in the bleachers and yell 'Good Eye.'"

Brian whirled around. "So that's all you think I do at these games?"

"Yeah," I said, my hands on my hips. "What are you gonna do about it?"

Brian opened his mouth to argue, then stopped. He stared

at his panting, sweaty wife, and started to laugh. Then he pulled me into a big bear hug. "I'll fight you later," he whispered. "Right now I think you need someone to hold you."

I growled and pushed against him, but he wouldn't let go. Finally I felt my muscles relax and I started to cry. Brian stroked my head. "I am such a stupe," I sobbed. "Oh, Brian, I feel so humiliated."

"Hey, Dad," Grayson said, bursting in and slamming the door. "Aren't we going to the game?"

"In a few minutes," Brian said. "I have to make a phone call first." Then he wiped my tears with his thumb. "I'll get the ward list."

"Thank you," I said. "I'm sorry for blaming you."

Brian smiled as he looked back at me and dialed. I listened as he smoothed things over with Brother Johansson, then I went into the living room and collapsed on the sofa as their conversation turned to our actual plumbing problems.

"He's coming over Saturday morning," Brian said as he headed out.

"What? No! I'll still be too embarrass—"

"Don't worry. You won't even be here," Brian said. "I'm sending you to get your nails done. Get a pedicure, the whole works, whatever you want."

I smiled. "You are wonderful."

"I know. And this time," he said as he headed out the door, "remember to shave your legs."

Just then Erica came downstairs, declaring her homework finished and double checked. "Okay," I sighed. "But then get right on piano practice. Sister Goodrow is coming over to meet with me about the ward talent show in about 45 minutes." Liz Goodrow was the ward activities chairman, and I had volunteered to coordinate this year's traditional extravaganza.

Last month I had prepared folders for her first meeting with the whole committee, and had watercolored hot air balloons on each one. Carefully beside each balloon I had written, "Reaching New Heights with the Activities Committee," then proudly shown my work to Brian.

"Perfect," he said. "Floating along with no propulsion and no sense of direction, just a blast of hot air."

"Brian!"

"What—you picked it," he said defensively.

I had sheepishly handed the folders out anyway, and another man on the committee had made a similar joke. Today, I hoped my meeting with Sister Goodrow would go more smoothly.

I went upstairs to freshen up, and soon I heard the familiar piano pieces Erica had been working on this week. She stopped for a few minutes, then I heard her begin again, only this time she was getting lazy, not using the proper rhythm and banging lazily on the keys.

"That sounds terrible!" I shouted down the stairs. "I can tell you're not reading the dynamics. And *count!*"

There was complete silence. I was about to shout, "Erica, can you hear me?" when suddenly she came down the hall from her bedroom towards mine.

I jumped. "What are you doing up here—and who's playing the piano?"

Erica looked mortified. "Sister Goodrow," she whispered. "She came in and asked if she could play, so I came upstairs."

I swallowed and shrank back into the bedroom, my knees buckling as I slumped into a chair. *How could I have said all those things to Sister Goodrow? That poor woman!*

My heart pounding, I hurried down the stairs. Sister Goodrow, I painfully remembered, had brought us a fabulous dinner when the triplets were born. She was now seated on the sofa, looking positively crushed.

"Oh, I am so sorry!" I said. "Please forgive me. I thought you were Erica." *(Oh, good, Andy. Tell her you thought she was your ten-year-old daughter who can play much better than she can.)* I mean, you really sounded fine. I just always tell Erica those things when she practices."

Sister Goodrow was still trying to smile through her humiliation.

"Oh, please forgive me," I said, giving her a hug. "I am so embarrassed."

Sister Goodrow smiled, then gave a little laugh. "I'll bet this is the most embarrassing thing you've done all day," she said. I smiled. Wait until she next chats with Sister Johansson, I thought. But I chuckled and nodded anyway.

"You're so prompt," I said.

Sister Goodrow shrugged. "I wasn't raised LDS."

Now we both laughed, then went to work on the final touches for the ward talent show, which was in two weeks.

When Brian and Grayson came back from baseball, I grabbed Brian's arm and pulled him into the coat closet.

"This is what I like about you—" he began, wiggling his eyebrows.

"Oh, stop it! That's isn't why I pulled you in here," I whispered.

"That isn't?"

"Cut it out," I snapped. "The triplets have ruined my brain, and now my grammar is a mess."

"I thought she was dead."

I snarled into Brian's grinning face. "I am not going to laugh at that ridiculous joke."

"Okay, so why are we in here?"

"I just humiliated myself again by criticizing Sister Goodrow when she tried to play the piano!" I began to cry.

Brian sighed as he held me in his arms. "Why did you do that?"

"It wasn't on purpose!" I hissed.

"Hey. Don't get mad at me. I was at a ball game. A *losing* ball game, I might add." Brian pushed hangers and coats aside to make more room.

"Well, if you had been home, none of this would have happened."

"Of course not."

I told Brian all about it.

He shook his head. "I'm going to have to lock you in here, aren't I?"

"How can I face either of them again?" I asked.

Brian kissed my forehead. "This too shall pass."

I hate that phrase. For one thing, it's always spoken to someone who's in a pot of hot water. And for another thing, it's always spoken to me.

That night Brian took over kidwatch and dinner duties since this was ward homemaking night. As I kissed him good-bye,

Brian whispered, "Now remember: Just don't say anything."

"You're such a help," I smirked. Then I kissed the children and left. It still felt funny driving to a Relief Society meeting and realizing that I hadn't been in on any of its planning. But it was also fun to walk in and be surprised, too. Little did I know how surprising the evening would become.

It was early December, so tonight was the big Christmas dinner. The whole room was decorated with bright poinsettias, garlands of holly, red tablecloths, and a huge nativity scene in one corner, borrowed from Monica.

In the center of each table was a white basket filled with favors (fragrant bundles of Christmas potpourri), and rising from each basket was a cluster of red and green helium balloons. True to their predecessors, this presidency was having a hard time simplifying, too.

I'm ashamed to admit it was with no small amount of relief that I glanced around and noticed that neither Sister Johansson nor Sister Goodrow was there—yet.

I sat at a table with some of the other sisters, and we marveled at the hard work that had gone into this special evening. Dinner was a classic feast of turkey, stuffing, cranberries, the works—with cake for dessert.

"How do you like the cake?" asked Lara Westin, my former homemaking counselor, as she walked by gathering plates.

"Delicious," I said.

She giggled and leaned closer. "I got the recipe from one of my catering books," she whispered. "It's called 'Better Than Sex' cake."

I was glad I didn't have a mouthful of it at the moment. "You don't say," I said.

I went to the rest room before the program began, and when I got back, a latecomer had taken my seat. No problem, I thought, I'll just sit at an empty table in the back. One of the sisters at my old table saw the awkward situation, but I waved away her concern. I was fine sitting by myself.

The show began with a cute skit of a family home evening. The grandmother in the play was telling her grandkids about Christmas on the farm when she was a child. "I still remember my father reading us 'The Night Before Christmas' as we gathered around the fireplace," she said. She then began to read this very poem to the children on the stage.

"'Twas the night before Christmas and all through the house, not a creature was stirring, not even a mouse,'" she said. All was perfectly quiet.

And then at that exact moment, for no reason I can imagine except that God does indeed have a sense of humor, one of the balloons at my table began hissing. LOUDLY. Heads whipped around, and just as suddenly as it had begun, the hissing stopped.

The grandmother in the skit glanced nervously out into the audience, then went on. Just as she came to the part about "there arose such a clatter" it happened again. Only this time it was even louder. I glanced around for a chair at another table. All of them were taken.

Again, women turned to stare. But none of them were looking at the culprit balloon; they were frowning at *me!* I knew they thought I was hissing at the performance, so to counteract what they were thinking, I began grinning and applauding.

"Isn't this great?" I mouthed silently to the nearest table.

The women frowned. Couldn't I see that the show hadn't ended yet? Why was I interrupting?

Feeling a blush that was red enough to glow in the darkened audience, I stopped clapping and returned my attention to the stage. By now the grandma was so rattled that her voice sounded like a shaky impersonation of Katherine Hepburn (frankly, it improved her performance). But I could see that she was not quavering on purpose; it was because she thought I was sitting there hissing at her, ready to start booing and throwing tomatoes.

Again the balloon began hissing, and two women turned to stare at me, holding a stern finger before their lips to shush me. Well! I was not going to sit there and be framed by a crummy little balloon—not after the miserable day *I'd* had! Impulsively, I leaped to my feet and began strangling one of the balloons at my table. It popped and everyone in the room jumped.

Still the hissing continued. I popped another one. Then another. I was a serial popper on a rampage.

Finally I ripped the last balloon in two, and the hissing stopped. Relieved and sweating, I smiled at the other sisters. *Now you'll see that it wasn't me,* I thought to myself.

But not one of them was smiling back. They were all staring at me in horror, including the grandma and children on stage.

I slumped into my chair, my table laden with the limp remains of red and green balloons, and the show continued. As I sat there, my heart pounding, I realized that maybe, just maybe, I had chosen the wrong course of action to stop the hissing.

By the time the skit had ended, a poem about the first Christmas had been recited, and half a dozen carols had been sung, I was able to reflect upon my actions and think of at least eight options I should have taken before attacking the centerpiece for embarrassing me.

Truly, I felt like the new Edith Horvitz. Forevermore, I imagined, people would smile at me with hesitant eyes, watch me walk a safe distance away, then whisper to a friend and shake their heads. "She's the one who murdered those balloons that Christmas," they'd say.

And stories of her mother going ballistic at homemaking night would undoubtedly mar Erica's adolescence and cost her the circle of friends that could lead to happy teen years, the desire to study, and ultimately, college admission. She'd be forced to hang out at 7-11 until she was thirty-five, at which point she'd marry a man so tattooed that his very race would be obscured by green ink.

After the show, I asked the new Relief Society president, Selma Neff, if I could *please* apologize into the microphone. Sister Neff was much older than I was, and somehow seemed softer or something. Everything about her radiated patience and understanding, from her gentle brown eyes to her grandma's hands that had kneaded a thousand loaves of bread. But my request was not on the program and it made her visibly nervous. Still, she was kind enough to give me a chance, and hesitantly stepped aside.

"I'm really sorry about what just happened," I said. Yikes—they think I'm apologizing for their amateur performances! I swallowed and started over. "I mean, for the hissing and then the popping at my table." Everyone was staring at me, wondering how I was planning to explain this one.

I took a deep breath. "A balloon—I don't know, maybe more than one—anyway, it started to leak."

"Andy," Sister Neff said, putting a loving arm around me, "the helium did this to you?"

"What? No!" I glanced at all the women whose eyes were now full of sympathy for their former Relief Society president, who had just succumbed to the effects of noxious gas.

"I thought it made your voice higher," somebody whispered.

This was going nowhere. "The balloon was making such a loud hissing noise," I said, "and I felt just terrible. I would never hiss at a church performance. I would never hiss *anywhere*." No, that wasn't true. "Actually, I would hiss if I went to a play and it turned out to be something immoral or offensive. No; I'd probably just leave. Actually, I would hope to know enough about the show before I got there—"

"Andy . . ." Sister Neff was pointing to her wristwatch.

I tried to find my way back to my original apology. "I did a very ridiculous thing," I said. "I didn't know how to stop the balloons from hissing, so I popped them. I know it sounds crazy, but I just felt . . . desperate. Anyway, it was very poor judgment and I am truly sorry."

Now the faces of the women were stretching into sympathetic smiles, and someone began clapping. Soon the whole room was nodding and clapping. I could feel my eyes filling with tears.

I started back to my table, then turned and grabbed the mike again. "I loved the program," I said. "I've always loved that poem, and those were some of my very favorite songs, and—"

"Thank you, Andy," Sister Neff said, gently taking the mike from me and guiding me off.

When I got home that night, Brian was sitting on the sofa, reading. "How'd it go?" he asked.

I sighed. "'Tis the season to be merry," I sang, "Blah blah blah blah blah, blah blah blah blah."

Brian put down a book about early Rome as I joined him on the sofa.

"What happened now?" he asked, putting a comforting arm around my drooping shoulders.

I told him the whole, humiliating story.

"But why would you do that?" he asked. "Didn't you realize that balloons popping would be much worse than hissing?"

I stared at Brian. With comfort like this, who needs gossips? "Well," I said, "usually I have a pistol with me for such occasions and I considered shooting the balloons instead, but then I thought that might be going over the line."

Brian held me and winced. "You've had the worst day."

"Thank you."

"You poor thing."

"That's right."

"You didn't even *say* anything this time." Brian sighed and looked into my weary face. "I am *so* glad I wasn't there," he said. Then he laughed.

"And to think I brought you some dessert."

Brian's eyes lit up. *"Pour moi?"*

I handed him a paper plate covered with a napkin. "It's called 'Better Than Sex' cake," I said.

Brian leaped to his feet. "I'll be the judge of that," he said as he headed into the kitchen. "They served 'Better Than Sex' cake for a Christmas dinner?" Brian took a bite of cake, then said, "Nope. Whose recipe is this?"

"Lara's."

Brian shook his head. "Poor Jerry."

"Poor Lara."

Then Brian laughed. "See? Your life could be worse."

I smiled and gave him a hug. "I'm so glad I have you," I said. "I couldn't have made it through a horrendous day like today, without you."

"Just think," Brian said, emptying a glass of milk. "We'll be together forever. You can embarrass yourself into the eternities. Won't it be funny if, when we die and we're greeted by all our ancestors, they all bring balloons?"

"Thanks for that cheery thought," I said. "I'll be sure to visit your comedy-free kingdom when I have some spare time."

CHAPTER 5

OUT OF THE MOUTH
OF BABES' MOTHER

On Saturday morning while Anders Johansson fixed our plumbing, I hid in a nail salon with my feet in a bucket of suds and my wet fingernails poised like claws before a portable fan. Occasionally I would straighten out my fingers and admire their glossy coral sheen. As a woman dried my feet and began snipping at my cuticles, I wondered if Brother Johansson had told anyone about my *faux pas,* or whether I could indeed show my face at church again.

Dr. Sanders had finally returned my call, and had concluded that my milk supply was dwindling due to stress. "What stress?" I said. "You mean being the mother of six kids, three of whom are triplet boys; the wife of the irrepressible Brian Taylor; a member of the activities committee for my church; head of three school committees; the sister of two women in therapy; and the patient of a doctor who won't call me back for three days? What's stressful about that?"

Dr. Sanders sighed. I knew he thought I was hysterical, but I figured he'd already concluded that much from our delivery room episode, so I had nothing to lose.

"Just try to take it easy," he said.

I didn't even mention that the lion's share of any stress I might be having was my own fault for the verbal gaffes that were becoming my trademark. What was all this hoopla over stress, anyway? Seemed like a trendy illness that should have outlived its popularity. Like hypoglycemia in the seventies; everybody and his parakeet had that one. Then it was cholesterol panic. And now stress had been hanging on, lining the pockets of self-help authors for what, fifteen years now? Just thinking about it raised my level of it. (As it turned out, the triplets were now eating so many other things that they were getting pretty tired of manna from Mama. After nine months they finally weaned themselves, and even my bruising disappeared).

When I got home from the nail salon (only after phoning to make sure Brother Johansson was gone), we got a call from the stake president, asking to meet with me and Brian. Now there was no doubt: word of my blunder had spread throughout the entire stake.

Lacking a baby-sitter, we packed up the kids and headed to the stake center. "Just tell him the truth," Brian whispered to me as we pulled into the parking lot. "I think it's a mistake anybody could make."

I frowned. "So how come I've made a string of these mistakes lately?"

Brian smiled and turned off the engine. "Andy, you're the mother of triplets who aren't even a year old yet. I think you're entitled to a few crossed wires. I mean, how many women could breeze through this experience without going a little crazy? Sleep loss alone—"

"I do feel like a zombie," I whispered back to him. "I stumble literally and verbally. I just wonder if I'm losing my mind."

Brian knew better than to tease me this time. "You're fine," he said. "These little goofs have shaken your confidence, but you need to remember what a bright, capable woman you are. You were Relief Society president! You saved Nick from terrorists, for heaven's sake. You're not an idiot."

I sighed. "Will you please tell President Palmer that I do *not* routinely ask men to look at my breasts?"

Brian gasped. "What—just on occasion?"

The older kids had already bolted into the stake center, so we buckled the triplets into their stroller, then told the entire bunch to be absolutely quiet in the hall.

Brian and I stepped nervously into the Stake President's office. And then, despite my growing reputation as the wife who can't keep from embarrassing herself for five minutes, President Palmer asked Brian to serve as first counselor in our new bishopric. Brian gulped with shock and fear; I sighed with relief and promised my full support.

"Let me tell you who your new bishop will be," President Palmer went on. Then, just as he was about to tell us, I could hear one of the triplets screaming.

"Oh, I am so sorry," I said, jumping up from my chair. "I'd better see what happened. I'll be right back," I called over my shoulder as I dashed from the room.

Austin had flipped himself over, even while buckled in his stroller seat, and had inched his way out of the stroller's leg hole until he was trapped by the armpits. Erica was frantically trying to free him, but nothing she and Grayson were trying could unwedge our little escape artist.

I pulled, I pushed, I soothed, I sang—Austin only screamed louder. After ten minutes, I finally dismantled the front bar and opened the leg hole so he could slide out. He fell into my arms, crying in little chokes as he wound down. Cameron and Bennett just stared (thank goodness; they usually take any brother's cry as a cue to harmonize).

Brian and President Palmer came out into the hall. "I figured you got tied up," Brian chuckled, examining my handiwork on the stroller.

President Palmer shook our hands, and we went home.

"Hey, wait a minute," I said as we walked in the front door. "Who's the new bishop?"

Brian smiled. "You snooze, you lose."

"Snooze? Excuse me?"

"Okay, you weren't snoozing. But I'm still not telling." Brian hugged me. "You'll get to find out along with everyone else tomorrow morning."

"No fair," I said, in the same whiny tones the kids use. But I knew better than to guess. Brian was determined to keep the secret.

That night as we were folding laundry (what else?), I reflected on the surprise this calling had been. I had always assumed that before a man is called to a bishopric or stake presidency, his wife's emotional state is carefully scrutinized for the virtue of stability. Frankly, I had never thought I'd pass inspection. "I guess it's just a rumor that they check out the wife first," I said.

"I guess so," Brian said.

I stopped in midfold. "What is that supposed to mean?"

"Hey, I try to be a nice guy," Brian said, placing a tiny little pair of shorts on a stack of play clothes. "When I disagree with you, you have a fit. So now I agree, and—"

"You always get it mixed up!" I protested. "And you do it deliberately."

A smug grin spread across Brian's cheeks as he continued to fold miniature socks into little balls. There was nothing left to do but swat him with a size 1 sweatshirt.

"Oh, yeah?" he said, eager to retaliate. He picked up a stack of clean diapers and flung them in my direction. They missed and fluttered all over the carpet.

Well, the fight was on. I wadded up a baby blanket and sailed it right into his chest. Now he returned my attack by firing a quick succession of sock balls that pummeled me like BBs.

Soon we were flinging every piece of laundry we could get our hands on, until both of us ran out of ammo and slumped laughing and exhausted onto the mountainous mess we had just created. Pieces of clothing were strewn over the whole room, a pant leg hanging from a lamp shade and tiny socks dotting the carpet like spilled popcorn.

"You are so childish," I said.

Now Brian came rolling over the top of me, pinning me down and tickling me until I admitted starting it. I looked up into his handsome face and we kissed. Then, reluctantly, we surveyed the damage.

"This will take forever to clean up," I sighed.

Brian held me in his arms and kissed me again. "Then let's take forever," he whispered. "I can't think of anyone I'd rather spend it with."

I hugged him, relishing the familiar feel of his chest and the curves of his face that fit my cheekbone perfectly.

"Just think of the things we used to worry about," Brian said, propping himself up on a pile of triplet-wear. "Everything seems so trivial now."

Just keeping up with the new babies had certainly adjusted my perspective. I remembered that my biggest fear a year ago was that someone in the Church would ask me, as ward Relief Society president, to help them dress a dead body. Of all the president's duties, that one scared me the most. *Now* my biggest worry was that *I'd* die—of exhaustion, probably—and someone else would dress me and see my flabby body before I could get my weight down again.

Actually, I found myself preoccupied with stretching our income, keeping the triplets healthy (we were averaging a doctor's visit a week), giving enough time to the older children when their hearts were full of joys and sorrows to share, helping with homework, cooking and cleaning for this many people, and trying to provide spiritual nourishment from what was sometimes a very depleted source.

There were too many days when I had let temporal concerns crowd out my scripture study. Then, when I needed to draw from the well for strength or wisdom, I was coming up with dry sand. I wanted desperately to keep my reserves replenished, so I'd have more of what matters most to offer my children.

But it was so *hard!* I mean, you can't send kids to school wearing nothing but good thoughts, can you? The harsh reality was that clothes had to be washed, floors cleaned, groceries bought, and I felt thrust into a graduate course on master planning and time management.

I had already hung a chart, labeled "Keep Mom Sane," on which I itemized household tasks and assigned names to each one. Amazingly, it was working (well, no promises on the sanity part). The kids were doing laundry, fixing certain meals and even bragging about their new skills to their friends. The initial grumbling over having to do all this stuff for free had eventually subsided as the kids recognized the crisis this really was, and that their help was truly needed. Brian and I were actually seeing a surge in their self-esteem as their competence grew in various skills.

But even with their help, it was still a madhouse most days.

We did so many loads of laundry and dishes that I fully expected a thank-you note from the gas company. If somebody were to ask me what I'd do differently if I discovered I were having triplets today, my answer would be to invest in companies that make baby wipes.

Brian traced my furrowed brow with the tip of his finger. "This isn't the life you signed up for, is it?" he asked sadly, as if he had personally shattered my dreams.

I looked around at the heaps of laundry, then up into the face of our new first counselor. "This is *exactly* the life I signed up for," I said, and kissed him. "It's just a little . . . more."

We laughed, then I touched his cheek. "I mean that, Brian. You are even more wonderful than I had hoped. The kids are more fun than I ever thought kids could be." I paused. "Of course it's more work right now. There are more trials than I would have asked for. But there are more blessings than I could possibly deserve. Everything's just . . . more."

"So you're happy?"

"Blissfully. How about you?"

"Semibliss with a chance of showers, clearing to scattered sunshine, followed by a beautiful weekend." He smiled and leaned back amidst the clothing. "That's Brian Taylor's Allegory of the Faithful Father. The symbolism means 'I'm usually happy despite this chaotic storm we're in, and I honestly believe we'll make it through raising the kids and eventually live happily ever after.'"

"Wake me for the ending," I said, and bunched a baby blanket under my head for a pillow.

"Okay," he yawned, and scooted close to hold me as we slept.

The following morning we were awakened by Erica shouting, "Whoa! What happened to you guys?" as she came upon the clothing-strewn battlefield.

"Oh," I said, still half asleep, "we were just folding some laundry . . ."

"And your mother decided to get into a clothes fight," Brian said.

"Did not," I mumbled, weakly lobbing a tiny shoe in his direction.

"I think I get the picture," Erica said. Then she disappeared into the kitchen.

Brian glanced at his watch and sighed. "We'd better get ready for church."

Grayson appeared in the hallway, his mouth agape at the explosion of laundry before him. "Boy, am I glad I don't have to clean *this* up," he said.

I shrugged. I guess my fleeting idea to make the clean-up an early family home evening would never have washed, anyway (pardon the pun).

I poked through the disarray for three outfits the triplets (who, thankfully, were still asleep) could wear to church. The clutter reminded me of Claudia Lambert (my friend with the pet pig whose house was so messy it made onlookers call the police), and I wondered if someone might look through my windows and think there'd been a burglary here, too.

At last, we collected enough items to attire three babies and packed the whole bunch into our eight-seater van.

As the kids and I sat beaming at him, Brian was sustained as first counselor in the new bishopric. Second counselor nearly made me faint—Jack Goodrow, Liz's husband! Surely he knew how rude I had been to Liz, accident or not; and now, how could I look at him up on the stand without wondering if he was thinking what a blockhead I was?

But the real shocker was when they announced the new bishop: Anders Johansson! I caught my breath and wondered if my heart had stopped. Tiny beads of sweat broke out all over my body, and Brian squeezed my shoulders. "Smile," he whispered in my ear.

I glued one on. "I'm going to die," I whispered back through my grinning teeth.

"No you're not," Brian whispered back. "He's the perfect choice, and he's the Lord's choice."

That wasn't my question. I had no qualms about Brother Johansson being a terrific bishop. My problem was *me!* How could I ever get past making such a fool of myself? And now he was the *bishop,* which somehow made matters worse. This meant he would be calling on the phone to talk to Brian, and I'd answer and he'd remember the last time we spoke on the phone (how could he not?) and I'd have to chuckle and act like a good sport (which I'm not), and then, in my nervousness, I'd probably say yet another stupid thing, and this would go on *ad infinitum.*

Tears were streaming down my face now, and Brian whispered, "Get a grip," into my ear.

The organist began playing "Nay, Speak No Ill" as I squeaked back at Brian, "He heard me say the word *breasts!*"

Brian shook his head and opened the hymn book. "I requested this song in your honor," he teased. "Everyone will be watching to see if you sing it."

I dug my fingers into his side. "That's not funny."

After the meeting, Edith came up to congratulate Brian and whispered, "If you had left that toupee on, I'll bet they would've made you the bishop!"

Later Brian was set apart, and I asked our new bishop if I could speak with him privately for a moment. Brian gave me a wink of encouragement and took the kids down the hallway.

Anders Johansson was a towering man with a broad, Swedish grin and a crushing handshake. He looked like he could throw a barn together in half an hour. Arnold Schwarzenegger should look so imposing. Bishop Johansson smiled and closed the door.

"I feel terrible," I said.

"What about?" Bishop Johansson asked, offering me a chair.

Did he have amnesia? Did he honestly not realize why I was shaking like a 7.2 on the Richter scale? I slid into the seat and stared at him. "Because of those things I said on the phone," I stammered.

Bishop Johansson gave me a reassuring smile and chuckled. "All forgotten," he said. "Besides, once Brian explained the misunderstanding, it was perfectly reasonable. Perhaps I should apologize to you for hanging up so abruptly."

I smiled and sighed. "Okay, so I don't have to run and hide every time I see you?"

"Not as long as you pay your plumbing bill." Bishop Johansson laughed. "Just kidding. Please don't let this bother you for another minute, Sister Taylor."

Whew. One down and one to go. I grabbed Jack Goodrow's sleeve in the hallway. "Jack, I need to speak with you," I said.

"Sure, Andy," he said. Jack was coach of everything, always ready to win-win-win. He was first to scamper up the trail on ward campouts, first up in the morning, period. Nothing slowed him down or dampened his spirits. If Jack were a beverage, he'd be carbonated Kool Aid.

We stepped into an empty classroom. "I have to get this off my breasts," I said. Then I gasped, and clamped my hands over my open mouth. "I meant off my chest," I said. But it was too late. Jack's eyes looked like Frisbees.

"I didn't mean to say that," I babbled a mile a minute. "I guess it was on my mind that I had said that to Brother Johansson, I mean Bishop Johansson—"

Now Jack was blanching and backing away.

"I can explain," I said, dissolving into tears and crying too hard to get the words out. Poor Jack stood there, not knowing whether to put a comforting hand on my shoulder or to run for his life. Nervously, he glanced out into the hallway.

"Brian?" he called.

"Jack?" Brian's voice—thank heavens. He came into the classroom and saw me sobbing and wiping tears with every available surface of my hands. "Andy—what happened?" He quickly directed Erica and Grayson to take the younger ones to the nursery and wait for us.

I tried to speak, but was still crying too hard. Brian looked to Jack for an explanation, but there was no way Jack was going to touch this one.

"Take a deep breath," Brian said, sitting me down on a folding chair.

My voice came out in little staccato bursts of hysteria. "I just wanted to apologize . . . for what I said to Liz the other day... and I ended up . . . saying breasts again."

Brian stared at me like I had truly lost it. "Why did you do that?" he asked.

"I meant to say chest."

This did not comfort Brian. "Why did you want to say chest?"

"Look, it's okay," Jack said. He had only been a member of the bishopric for ten minutes, I thought, and already he was lying.

"It is not okay," I said. "I was trying to get something off my chest. I didn't want to be embarrassed every time I saw you or Liz. I said a dumb thing to her the other day and I didn't want you to always think of that."

"So you said breasts to get his mind off the first thing?" Brian was absolutely flabbergasted.

"Of course not!" I said. "I said breasts when I meant chest."

Brian was still shaking his head, thoroughly confused.

Now Jack was stifling a chuckle, evidently realizing what was happening. "Liz did tell me about the piano thing," he said. "But she thought it was funny. Her feelings aren't hurt and we aren't judging you, Andy."

"So now I only have to worry about what just happened in here."

Jack shook his head again. "No you don't."

I turned to Brian. "I'm the ward buffoon, aren't I?"

"Of course not," he said, holding me to him. Eleven minutes and now he was lying, too.

"I wish Edith Horvitz would invent something to keep my mouth shut," I mumbled.

"She did," Brian said.

"I did *not* mean to glue it," I said.

"You just need some sleep," Brian said, stroking my head.

Jack chuckled as we all went out into the hall. "Andy," he said, just as I was feeling a little better, "this too shall pass."

CHAPTER 6

THROUGH A VALE OF CHEERS

The first Friday in January was not only the ward talent show, but Nick and Zan's due date as well. Nick, ever the daring soul, had agreed to emcee, with former Bishop Carlson standing by to fill in if Zan should go into labor. "Don't worry," I told Zan, as she sat nervously on an aisle for a speedy exit, "nobody has their baby on their actual due date. I think it's the law or something."

"However," Brian cautioned her, "you might want to rethink doing a gymnastics routine for the show."

Zan smiled. "Oh, darn. And I was so hoping to do one."

Just then Edith Horvitz entered the cultural hall. My stunned expression made both Brian and Zan turn to stare. "Who is that—Zorro?" Brian whispered.

Now, like dominoes, our kids' heads snapped around to stare.

"Shhh," I said. No one needed to explain that this was Edith. She was decked out from head to foot in black leather, including a leather cowboy hat.

"Are those studs or sequins?" Zan asked.

"Studs, I think," I said. Actually, I knew. She recently told me that as a tribute to Elvis, who never wore sequins—only studs—that she, as a rising rock star, would do the same.

"Thought I'd give everybody a sneak preview of my next album," Edith said. "They've heard me sing the hits of the sixties, so tonight I'm gonna do a couple of seventies tunes."

Tunes? She's saying tunes, now, instead of songs?

"She looks like a biker," Erica whispered to me as we all sat down. I motioned her not to say any more.

Edith sat beside me as the show began, since her bit wasn't scheduled until later. The first act was a hilarious skit starring Lara as a homemaking mini-lesson teacher. Wearing glasses as thick as binoculars and lisping through a set of wax teeth, she pretended to teach a group of three sisters how to crochet. But the more she explained, the more confusing it got. Soon she was wrapping great clumps of yarn around her hands, while the other sisters were getting tangled in one another's work as they tried to help each other.

Finally Lara went over to them and reached into the fray (literally) until they were all so knotted together that two sisters fell off their chairs, pulled Lara on top of them, and the whole bunch rolled offstage entwined in yarn, like bugs in a giant spider web. For every sister who has ever felt inept in a handiwork class, this skit was a major hoot. Even Edith, Queen of Crochet and the single largest consumer of yarn in this country, loved it.

Next, three laurels performed a classical number on flute, piano and violin that was just beautiful. I turned to Erica and whispered, "Aren't they terrific?" Erica sighed. "You are totally transparent, Mom." Okay, so I was hoping Erica would find some inspiration here to practice the piano.

The laurels were followed by a deacon who did a magic act using his younger siblings as assistants. It was a sermon in patience as he politely watched the toddlers botch every one of his carefully planned tricks.

Next a teenager came out and sang some Jewish songs he'd prepared for a friend's bar mitzvah. Obviously duplicating the act to the letter, he even shouted, "Everybody!" before one chorus. *Everybody?* We all smiled and tried our best to follow his lips.

Then the new bishopric (spurred on by Brian, the former choir director) sang a cute version of "Be Our Guest" from *Beauty and the Beast,* reworking the lyrics to describe their eagerness to serve ward members.

Next up was eighty-seven-year-old Luther Dunlap, doing a sprightly tap dance to "Yankee Doodle." He really looked sensational in white tie and tails; walking onstage, he brought a round of applause. Starting slowly, he introduced tougher and tougher steps that brought cheering each time—right up to the smashing conclusion, when he actually jumped into the air and came down in perfect splits! Then he bowed over in a dramatic finish as the crowd leaped to its feet in applause.

On and on we clapped, as Luther held his final pose. At last the cheering faded and a few voices were heard saying, "Wonderful!" and "Fantastic!" as we sat back down. But Luther was still holding his difficult pose, so we rose to our feet again for one final ovation. Luther obviously wanted a bigger thank-you, and we didn't mind giving him one; his act had been tremendous.

Again, the applause faded and we sat down. Luther still wasn't moving. Nick went on stage to pat him and politely move things along; but when Luther ignored him, he took hold of Luther's shoulders and gently shook him. "Luther?" he said. Luther's head wobbled.

Immediately more brethren hurried onstage, one of them the veterinarian, Brother Patterson. Brother Patterson suddenly turned back to the audience and shouted, "He's expired!"

A collective gasp rose from the crowd, then a roar of confusion. Someone called an ambulance as the members mobilized in lying Luther down, shooing away curious children, and calling his next of kin. Folks were visibly shaken, some crying and others muttering embarrassed comments about how awful it was that we all just stood there clapping like fools.

Just then a woman's voice rose up over the pandemonium and screamed, "NICK!" All fell silent as we turned. It was Zan and she was clutching her belly in pain.

"Breathe! Breathe!" A dozen women clustered around her, each one coaching her in a different method of childbirth.

"Get some hot water!" one shouted.

"Get some towels!" another shouted.

"Get out of the way!" Nick boomed, pushing his way through the crowd and pulling Zan from the reluctant clutches of the would-be midwives. Then Nick and Zan hurried from the building, Nick pale as a pillowcase.

Thirty seconds later an ambulance came screeching up to

the doors, and paramedics ran into the room. The frenzy of confusion among the rest of us was dissolving into organized retreat, as various priesthood leaders began calming and directing the crowd.

Obviously the talent show was over.

"Gee, you sure plan great activities," Brian whispered in my ear. "Never a dull moment."

"Hush," I whispered. "Trust you to make matters worse." I glanced at Liz Goodrow, who looked frozen in shock as she watched our plans disintegrate before her eyes. "I'd better talk to her," I said, and went over to where she was standing.

"Isn't this awful?" I whispered to Liz.

"Just terrible," she agreed.

"I'm sorry," I said.

Liz smiled. "Andy, you are the only person I know who would actually take responsibility for a death and a birth." She gave me a big hug. "There was nothing you could have done."

I smiled and squeezed her hand. After a closing prayer, we all headed out to the parking lot.

"So did she fire you?" Brian whispered. I elbowed him to be quiet.

"I can't believe it!" Edith bellowed. "Now I don't get to do my act!"

I stepped between Edith and Erica so that Edith wouldn't see Erica's open mouth and rolling eyes.

"Should we go to the hospital?" Grayson asked Brian.

But Edith interrupted. "Oh, it's no use, honey. He's dead as a doornail."

"He meant to see Nick's and Zan's baby," Brian said, mustering all the patience he could.

"Now isn't that a coincidence?" Edith chuckled. "One pops into the world as another checks out!"

I sighed, and decided to answer Grayson's question. "I think we'll wait until Nick calls us," I said, scooping the triplets out of their stroller and placing them in their car seats. We bid goodnight to Edith and got into our van.

"Poor Luther," I said as we drove along.

"Well . . ." Brian said, "you've got to admit, it was a great exit."

"Brian!"

"It was. He left this life to a standing ovation. How many people can go out in that much glory?"

I just glared at him. First I had to endure Edith's analysis of the evening, and now Brian's.

"Some glory," Erica said. "Being pronounced dead by a *vet*."

"Not even dead," Grayson said, "but *expired*. That's even worse. It makes him sound like a fishing license."

"Grayson!" I said. Couldn't anybody in this family show a little respect for the dead?

"Or a subscription to *Newsweek*," Erica laughed.

"No, no!" Ryan said, gleefully joining in. "A subscription to *Life!*"

Now Brian and all the kids burst into hysterics, and I was ready to throttle every one of them. Even the triplets were giggling.

"Hey," Ryan said, "is it true that when you die, you get to see the world?"

Oh, great, I thought. More false doctrine from the Mormon rumor mill.

"Yeah, right," Erica sneered. "Just as you die and your family is sobbing around your bed, you take off to catch the last game of the World Series."

"Then from there," Brian joined in, oblivious to the fact that he was a *parent* in this picture, "you figure, why not zip by Hawaii for a couple of acts at the Polynesian Cultural Center?"

Grayson leaned back, folding his arms in satisfaction over his chest. "Kick the bucket and see the world," he sighed.

Two hours later Monica called. "Wasn't it just horrible?" she asked. "I hope Brittany doesn't have nightmares. I mean, what a terrible experience for a child to have."

I agreed, and decided not to share the fact that my own kids were laughing and having a pillow fight in the next room, this event having supplied them with joke material for an entire week.

On Saturday morning we got a call from the hospital. Nick and Zan were now the parents of an eight-pound boy! Zan did beautifully through a very long labor, and was now recovering and ready for visitors. They named him Nolan, and we dashed right over to welcome our new little relative to the world.

"I still think they should have had the baby at the ward," Grayson said. "He could have been delivered by a veterinarian."

"That would've been cool," Ryan agreed.

I threw my arms around Nick—my little baby brother was a daddy! I was bursting with joy. And Nolan was darling—a blue-eyed brunette just like Zan, with eyelashes you could see from twenty feet away.

Zan was exhausted but thrilled. She could hardly hold back the tears of joy as she cradled her own little son. And Nick was bouncing off the walls like a ping-pong ball. "Isn't he great?" he kept saying.

My mother and sisters showed up, looking more fatigued than Zan. "All these babies," Natalie sighed to me in the hallway, as if she herself had given birth to them.

"I guess we won't be able to have Thanksgiving together if this keeps up," my mother whispered.

"It's only one for Nick and Zan," I reminded them. "Please don't say such things around them." How could they not rejoice at the arrival of a sweet little baby?

Zan's parents arrived with Wanda, her sister. Irving studied his little grandson through the nursery window. "He's an Archer," he announced. Olive nodded and Wanda smiled her approval.

"He was cute, but it seems like they got gypped—only one baby," Grayson said as we headed home.

"Maybe we could give him one of ours!" Ryan piped up. I glared him back down again.

"Maybe I'll get to baby-sit," Erica, now eleven, said, her eyes twinkling with dollar signs.

The next day, Brian was asked to conduct the funeral for Luther Dunlap. Bishop Johansson had won a big plumbing bid, and had to get his workmen started on the Tuesday morning of the funeral.

Despite being a professor and giving lectures for a living, Brian was a nervous wreck. The solemnity of the situation, the pressure not to fluff it on such a serious occasion, had him almost shaking.

As he was preparing his remarks on Sunday evening, Erica walked in from a visit at a friend's house. "Mom, I can't believe what I just heard about you."

I sighed. I knew the balloon story would sift down to the ward youth eventually. "Well, good," I said, sitting down to entertain the triplets. "You'd be in a sorry mess if you believed everything you heard."

"I mean," she said, elongating the word *mean* as if I was too thick to understand a normal cadence, "what you did at home-making night." Erica would make a good principal at a home for delinquent girls.

I looked up and smiled. "Go on." I was wondering how this story had shaped up through its various tellings.

"You, like, totally smashed up a centerpiece and knocked over chairs? Come *on!* It's like you and Sister Horvitz both think you're rock stars or something."

I kind of liked this version better than the actual story. I sighed. "Well, what can I say? I've been growing more like Edith every day." I put a sock puppet on my hand and pretended to gobble the triplets' toes.

Erica snorted, her hands on her hips. "I am, like, totally embarrassed."

Well, what else was new? Embarrassment seemed to be Erica's emotion of choice these days, and certainly this tale did nothing to alter that course.

Brian, overhearing this exchange, called her into the dining room where he had notes and scriptures spread out on the table. "As I heard it, your mother did nothing of the sort. Some balloons were hissing at her table, so to keep from interrupting the show, she popped them. That's all."

Now Erica wheeled around, more horrified than ever. "You *what?*"

"No big deal," Brian shrugged, still trying to downplay the event for me.

"What did it sound like—gunshots?" Erica asked.

"Cool—there were gunshots? Where?" Grayson asked, wandering in from the kitchen.

"There were no gunshots," Brian said, like Colin Powell at a press conference during Desert Storm.

"Mom, how could you?" Erica's voice was filled with rage and humiliation. Clearly, I had destroyed her life.

"Erica," I said. "A minute ago you thought I had trashed the entire room, but now that you know it was only a couple of balloons, you're outraged?"

"Because that's . . . just . . ." she was groping for a polite word, but couldn't find one. "Stupid!" she finally blurted. Then she quickly apologized. "I'm sorry. I know we don't say that word, but—" She shrugged, as if to say, "But that's the only word that fits!"

"You know," I said, trying desperately to remember the Church's parenting course about not discounting, belittling or decking your kids, "you weren't there, and you don't know the whole story. As a matter of fact, I apologized to the sisters for disrupting the program."

This washed over Erica like a negligible breeze. "But what on earth made you think of popping them?" She stared at me as if she couldn't possibly share one chromosome with me.

"Erica, you have no right to challenge your mother's judgment," Brian said. "As she just said, you weren't there."

"I am so *glad,*" she said, eyes rolling wildly again as she imagined the incomprehensible scene.

"I'd still like to know why it would have been better to smash a centerpiece," I said, "than to pop a couple of balloons."

Erica made gagging sounds as she exhaled. These gagging sounds were meant to emphasize that her upcoming answer was obvious to all but the moron asking the question. "Well, that's embarrassing because it's, like, you're trying to be cool even though you're too old," she said. "But at least there would be a reason!"

Ah. I knew there was a logical explanation. "You do know," I said, "that this kind of behavior skips a generation, and that while you would *never* do something so ridiculous as to pop a balloon in public, your children will. In fact, they'll probably do it during your inaugural address when you become president."

Erica smirked. "Ha ha. Even if I wanted to run for president I couldn't, because you guys would embarrass me to death." She stomped off to her room.

I turned to Brian. "You know," I said, "that would only be fair. After all, kids spend their childhood embarrassing their parents, right? How many times did she throw up all over me just before I had to teach a Spiritual Living lesson? And how many visiting teachers did she poke in the stomach and ask if there was a baby in there? And what about the time she told the loan officer at the bank that he had bad breath? And—"

"I know," Brian said. "I guess it's that adolescent phase.

You didn't really expect her to sympathize with you, did you?"

"Well, no," I admitted. "But she honestly thinks we're stupid, Brian. Me, anyway."

"And old," he added.

"Gee, thanks. I forgot that one."

Brian came over and hugged me.

I looked up at him and said, "If you tell me 'this, too, shall pass' I'm going to slug you."

The night before his big funeral debut, Brian decided to teach a family home evening lesson on the topic foremost on his mind: death.

The triplets, of course, were romping happily in their play zone, but the older three just stared at Brian the way you'd look at a newsreel on the spread of fungus.

Somehow the lesson took a turn toward the medical, and as Brian listed various causes of death (an unnecessary element of his lesson, he later conceded), the kids' faces grew longer and longer. Ryan kept stopping him to explain what each disease entailed, and by the end of the evening Erica and Grayson were thoroughly disgusted.

"I'd like to get to the hereafter," Brian said, at length.

"Me too," Erica said, willing to die to get out of this lecture.

Brian sighed. "I meant that I'd like to explain about the

hereafter." His eyes narrowed at his daughter. "The plan of salvation is very exciting."

Now nobody would believe him, after his depressing prelude. "Unfortunately, we're out of time," he said, aware that the older three had school in the morning.

I tried to smile and look encouraging, as if the lesson had gone beautifully. I knew Brian was nervous about tomorrow's funeral. But I couldn't help wondering which of our kids would creep into our room tonight with nightmares.

As they ate chocolate ice cream, which they shaped into tombstones with their spoons, Brian whispered, "Maybe I'll just skip to the plan of salvation at the funeral tomorrow. Make it a little more upbeat."

I smiled. I could only imagine the pallor of gloom that would hang over the services if he didn't.

The next morning Brian paced in his black suit, rehearsing and practicing his speech.

"Honey," I said, "I don't think there will be that many people there." Brother Dunlap was a widower with no living relatives that any of us knew. We figured a sprinkling of ward members would be all who'd show up.

Brian stopped in his tracks and reminded me that "if you only have one sheep, you still feed it."

I smiled. "Well, you'll do great," I said.

I slid into a bench near the back of the chapel where I could beat a hasty retreat with the triplets if necessary. They were napping in their stroller now, but that could change abruptly.

Luther's home teacher spoke first, giving us a blow-by-blow account of all Luther's eighty-seven years. Next, a singer from the mortuary sang a couple of long, drowsy numbers; and the next thing I knew, one of the triplets was fussing and waking me up.

Startled, I sat bolt upright and stared ahead. Brian was just finishing his talk on the plan of salvation. And he was staring straight at me.

I managed a smile and blinked my eyes. Austin was building to a crescendo, so I picked him up and tried to quiet him.

Now Cameron began waking up, then Bennett, and soon I had to wheel the entire bunch wailing out of the chapel.

As soon as Brian came out into the parking lot I rushed over to him. "Listen, I—"

"Oh, no you don't," Brian said, holding up his hand like a policeman stopping traffic. "Don't try to worm your way out of this one, my dear." Then he leaned into my face and hissed, "You fell asleep! My first funeral speech and you slept through the entire thing!"

"Not the entire thing," I squeaked, knowing I was without excuse.

"My own wife." Brian was determined to say his piece on this subject, so I listened and took my licks. "I must have worked on that talk for eight hours," Brian continued. "And you fell asleep." He shook his head.

"It was the singer's fault," I said. "She was so soporific."

Brian opened his mouth to continue his tirade, then stopped. "Soporific?"

I grinned. Finally—a word he didn't know. "That's right," I said. "And idiopathic." I looped my arm through Brian's. "So was it a good speech?"

Brian sighed. "Disastrous. Not a wet eye in the house."

"You are so *funny,*" Sister Neff said, patting Brian's arm as she walked past.

I turned to Brian. "You gave a funny speech at a funeral?"

"Well, I didn't want to leave everyone depressed like I did for family home evening," Brian said. "I guess I went a little too far the other way."

"Hey, Brian," Cam Verne, the elders' quorum president, called out, "Great talk! They ought to invite you to speak at General Conference."

Brian smiled and whispered to me, "Right. The Monday session."

CHAPTER 7

LOOSE SLIPS SINK SHIPS

"There's something you need to know about boys, Mom," Grayson said to me one day as he was helping me pull clean clothes from the dryer.

This is good information, I thought to myself. It's about twenty years late, as I could have used such knowledge during my high school years and saved myself a good bit of confusion. However, better late than never. I was all ears.

"They don't wear tops," Grayson announced.

Earth shattering. I just stared at him for amplification. None came. So I pulled one of the triplets' examples from the dryer. "Then what do you call this?" I asked him.

"That's a *shirt*," Grayson clarified. "Girls wear tops."

I paused. "I see. What if it isn't cut in shirt style, and just has, say, a wide neck?"

Grayson stared at me as if no self-respecting boy would dream of wearing such an item.

"Shirts imply a certain cut," I went on. "Buttons down the front and a collar." They were decidedly different from pullovers, blouses, or even tops.

Grayson was shaking his head, almost in pity at my ignorance. "Boys wear shirts," he said. This was obviously etched in stone. "And," he said, "they don't have bangs."

The triplets were nearly two now, and they were finally growing enough hair that I had this morning commented about their needing haircuts. I might have said something about bangs.

"No bangs?" I asked. "Then what do you call the hair in front?"

"The hair in front," Grayson said, with an unspoken "duh" at the end of his sentence.

I smiled. "And you're content to live your life without a specific name for this part of your hair that you comb every day."

Grayson held his palms up on either side and said, "I rest my case." He'd been resting his case a lot these days, now that he was ten and out of those babyish single digits. Brian and I were finding ourselves his unwitting pupils every time he decided we needed some enlightenment about the world in general.

"You're going to be an interesting adult," I said.

Grayson grinned exactly like Brian. "Of course—I'm already an interesting kid."

Couldn't argue with that.

Erica was twelve now, and still swinging precariously back and forth between childhood and adolescence. She would go to bed as Erica Our Honey and wake up as Erica The Hun.

Ryan was seven, and by all counts, hyperactive. "It isn't enough that we had triplet boys," I said to Brian. "We had to have another son whose idea of bedtime is sometime the following morning." Ryan had been diagnosed as having Attention Deficit Disorder, despite my protests that this was the next trendy ailment to follow on the heels of stress.

Still, there was no denying that a kid who can't remember to turn off a water faucet, to tie his shoes, to come back when sent to his room for a sweater, or to put the milk in the refrigerator (as opposed to the cupboard), is possibly not paying the keenest of attention. Since preschool his teachers had complained of his daydreaming, and once we had ruled out seizures and hearing problems, I was certain he was a genius so bored with the mundane tasks around him that he was choosing to tune out. Then the triplets came along, and I figured Ryan was just losing his mind like his mother.

But by the time he was seven, I was ready to beg the pediatrician for medication (for Ryan or for me, at that point I didn't care which). I was hoping for a miracle, but we settled for slight improvement.

It still took every ounce of patience Brian and I could muster to gently guide Ryan through his chores, keeping him on track. He was still as lovable as ever, but completely unable to follow through without our help.

And, of course, it became a full-time career to read books and attend seminars on how to raise an ADD child. We discovered we had to learn entirely different parenting techniques for Ryan. Even his schoolwork had to be modified because we discovered that Ryan also had dysgraphia. "Dis *what?*" I had asked. Turns out it's similar to dyslexia, only instead of having reading problems, Ryan had trouble writing. It was extremely difficult for him to write numbers or letters (and imagine school without them). He knew the answers in his mind, but they couldn't flow from his fingers, so his schoolwork was slow, laborious and often illegible. Again, we delved into further research and legal hearings to allow Ryan to dictate his homework, type, and use a tape recorder when possible.

"How can you have a child with ADD and dysgraphia?" Natalie asked me one afternoon on the phone. "I mean, didn't you have enough to do already?"

"What, you think there's some computer doling all this out evenly among the population?" I asked. I could just picture somebody saying, "Nope—can't send the Taylors any more worries; they have triplets, you know."

"I just know *I* could never handle it," Natalie said. Again, she reiterated her gratitude at still being single and free from the horrendous life she saw me living.

I laughed. "First of all, I'm so happy I could split my sides," I said, stretching the truth just a tad on some days, "and second of all, you could probably handle more than you think."

"No way," Natalie said. "And I hope God is listening."

Natalie couldn't see how smug I looked when I said, "I'm sure he is." Just wait, Natalie, I thought. Your time will come.

Meanwhile, the triplets were dismantling the kitchen, so I hung up and ran to the crime scene, only to see them unloading the cupboards and the refrigerator. Ketchup and salad dressing had been squirted into every clean pot they could find, and Austin was using a celery stalk to bang on a cookie sheet. Can you believe I came upon this scene and actually felt relieved that at least the boys were all in one place?

While the first year was a blur, this second one was a whir. Everything felt as if it were in motion. There seemed to be toddlers everywhere, all noisy, all wanting attention at the same time. Their speech was delayed in the beginning, because they would hear each other's baby sounds and copy them. But they also learned to walk early, and never in the same direction.

"If we put flares on their ankles, they could look like fireworks, shooting out from the same starting place," Grayson observed.

"Probably, but let's pass on that idea," I yawned.

The words "baby proof" were simply not applicable. We needed our house to be "triplet proof" and found that with each passing day, that was a state not easily attained. They somehow knew to combine their reasoning powers and collectively think of ways around every obstacle I could construct. They even climbed on each other's backs to scale the baby gates.

When they were two and a half, I witnessed the first tantrum in triplicate that has—I think—ever been staged in the detergent aisle of a supermarket. Each one of them wanted me to put a different soap into the cart. (Imagine even having a preference at two-and-a-half! No one can accuse the Taylors of not watching enough television.) And when I refused to pay three times the price for half the soap, they—junior economists, all—went nuts. I had to drag them bodily from the scene (three kids, two hands, you figure it out) and take them home.

Nick and Zan's little Nolan, of course, was the perfect child. Inquisitive but charming, Nolan never painted their car, never smeared peanut butter on Zan's legs, never did any of the things my kids think are family traditions. He wasn't even one yet, but already he could sit quietly through an entire sacrament meeting (something my own husband cannot master).

"Don't feel bad," Monica said to me one Sunday as I was once again dragged into the nursery to calm a wailing triplet. "Some people get into the terrible twos and never find their way out!"

The good news was, after chasing three toddlers I had lost my excess weight and was now back to my normal size. The bad news was, I didn't realize how thin I had become until I completely embarrassed myself during a testimony meeting.

I had dressed hurriedly (is there any other way?), pulling on a half-slip that I'd worn just after having the triplets. It was something like size Jumbo Gigantic. But, hey, I figured it had an elastic waistband, so who would know the difference?

Then, I was standing at the podium about to bear my testimony, when suddenly the slip fell to my ankles like a dropped curtain. Erica later told me that the mouths of the entire bishopric fell open and their eyes nearly popped out. Of course, only those on the stand knew why; but unfortunately, Brian was on the stand.

I glanced down, saw my slip on the floor, and froze for a second. *How can this have happened?* I cried silently to myself. I took a big breath, stepped out of the slip, and squatted down to pick it up. In my nervousness, I wrapped it over and over my hands as I stood there and tried to complete my remarks. Then I bolted for my seat. I glanced at Brian, whose eyes were rolling in different directions. I offered him a weak smile. He shook his head, snickering.

After the meeting, he seemed clearly amused by the variety of ways in which his wife could embarrass herself. "Why did you do that?" he asked.

"I didn't do anything," I said, trying to conceal my anguish in a whisper. "The slip did it."

"Why did you wear such a big slip?" He looked at me as if I were a curiosity at a sideshow.

"Because it used to fit! How was I to know—"

"Why did you pick it up and wave it?"

"I did not wave it! I held it," I hissed back at him. "And what was I supposed to do, leave it there on the floor?"

"It was almost as if you were losing weight right before my

eyes. Like time-lapse photography," Brian marveled.

I tried to look tough and snarled, "Like I planned it! I am embarrassed to death and all you can do is poke at the body and say, 'Hmm . . . wonder how this one died . . .'"

"But it was so amazing . . ." he went on.

"Right in front of the bishop and Jack Goodrow!" I winced.

Brian sighed, "Well, we can't go back in time."

"If we could, we'd have to go back to my birth," I said, "because that's when I began this sojourn into continual embarrassment."

Brian smiled and gave me a long hug, then kissed me on the neck. "So," he whispered, "is it true that you're not wearing any underwear?"

I slapped his arm. "You are incorrigible. How come things like this never happen to you?"

"Well," Brian said, "for one thing, I don't wear slips."

"You know what I mean," countered. "You never embarrass yourself.

"Sure I do. Remember the choir seats?" Years ago, Brian had bought stadium seats at a discount and donated them to a fledgling branch. A week later he was mortified to discover the reason they were so cheap: they had "Joe's Plumbing Supply" printed on them.

"That doesn't count," I said. "You basically never embarrass yourself."

Brian smiled. "Come on, I'm not perfect. I do have one idiosync."

"*One* idiosync?" I laughed. "Well, that's good to know, darling. And it was very big of you to admit it."

CHAPTER 8

A BEDTIME LULLABY

It wasn't long before the triplets began toilet training, an experience akin to housebreaking an entire litter of puppies. Again, I bravely ventured into the supermarket—this time with Grayson in tow—and made the colossal mistake of turning my back on them near the dairy case.

"Austin, no!" I heard Grayson scream.

I turned around and saw Austin's bare bottom, his pants around his ankles and his shirt pulled up to his neck. He was proudly standing before the milk cartons, doing what comes naturally and, no doubt, anticipating Mommy's delight now that he'd become a big boy.

There were so many shoppers staring—all aghast, as you might expect—that I gave serious thought to apologizing over the intercom.

Grayson was standing there, shaking his head, and copied the line Brian had been using with increasing frequency: "This is gonna put me under."

Me first, I thought.

We had held a family council months ago, all pledging to do whatever it took to help one another, especially since Ryan had to dictate an hour's worth of homework to me every night. If a triplet needed changing or feeding, the older kids knew simply to *do* it, not to call for Brian or me. And they had been pretty good about rallying together for the sake of survival.

But watching Grayson grow pale beside the dairy case, I knew I couldn't ask him to hand me some Lysol and paper towels. This was above and beyond. So I gave him the grocery list and asked him to please find the cheapest and biggest of everything, while I cleaned up after the triplets (two of whom were about to follow Austin's lead).

Brian was home when we got back from the supermarket. He bounded out onto the porch to welcome us home.

"Sure, *now* you're home," I sneered, hefting cases of soup onto a dolly and wheeling it past him into the house. "Do you realize that suddenly everything we buy comes in a drum? We don't carry in groceries anymore! No, that would be too normal. *We* load huge bulk items onto an industrial dolly. Maybe we should get a forklift."

Brian turned to Grayson. "What happened to her at the store?"

Grayson shook his head. "Trust me, Dad. You don't want to know."

Brian took the boxes from me as I was unloading them, then guided me by the shoulders to a sofa. "I should get a job as a dock worker," I went on, building a good pout. "I'll bet my biceps are the largest of any woman's in the ward."

Brian stared into my face. "I don't know what happened, but I'm sure you'll tell me eventually. Meanwhile, just sit here and relax. I'll unload everything."

"You'll get a hernia," I mumbled.

Brian sniffed the air. "What's that I smell—a new perfume?"

"Essence of Ipecac," I said. "That's all I ever smell like anymore. That, or baby wipes."

"No, no," Brian said, filling his lungs and trying to guess. "It smells like pine or something."

"Pine Sol," I growled. "And I don't want to talk about it."

Grayson, unfortunately, did. He told the entire story in lurid detail, until Brian doubled up laughing, glancing now and then at me to make sure I was registering the proper degree of defeat.

Finally, having laughed himself into a state of semigenuine pity, he came over and snuggled me on the sofa.

"If I don't have a piece of pie within the next two hours," I said, "I cannot be held responsible for my actions."

"Erica," Brian called.

She came in beaming. She had been baby-sitting Ryan and helping him with his homework. "All done!" she crowed. "I wrote the best poems for Ryan! He is gonna get an A."

"That was not what I meant by helping him with his homework," I said. "You were supposed to do the *writing* only."

Erica laughed and shrugged. "I did! I wrote him some poems. Wanna hear them?"

"Let Ryan *dictate* the poems to you," Brian said.

Erica scowled. That was not nearly so fun.

"And please watch the triplets while I take your mother out for a piece of pie. I think it's a matter of life and death."

"Oh, she's not gonna die," Grayson scoffed, as if there were no such luck.

"No, but some of *us* might," Brian chuckled.

"Remember the balloon massacre," Ryan warned Grayson. This had become a family motto, not unlike "Remember the Alamo," and served to remind them all of Mom's unstable mental state.

Brian helped me into a jacket. "We'll be back in thirty minutes, kids. Be good."

I kicked at a stack of newspapers in the garage as Brian and I headed to the car. "The kids need to recycle," I said.

"Into what?" Brian asked.

I laughed. "Won't it be wonderful when they're all toilet trained?"

"Toilet trained?" Brian said as we backed out. "I was thinking how great it will be when they're all grown and married!"

I sighed. "I do love them, I really do. But . . ."

"You've had a rough day," Brian said. "This is a pie day."

"Every day's a pie day, then."

"I'll go for that."

I laughed and scooted up next to him. All through dessert we giggled and flirted, *almost* forgetting that we were due back home in 30 minutes. It was exactly the break I needed.

On the way home, I twirled my fingers through Brian's hair (what hair he has) and nibbled on his ear. Instantly, Brian pulled over and turned off the engine. He drew me into a passionate embrace and kissed me. Just as we were steaming up the windows, he pulled back. "Why are we doing this?" he asked. "Why don't we just hit ourselves over the heads with a hammer? This can't go anywhere!"

He was right. For one thing, we were parked in front of the Lesbitt's house, neighbors who had probably already called the police. And for another thing, we were due home five minutes ago.

"Well," I said, smoothing my hair into place, "it was a fun idea."

Brian smiled and started up the engine. "Hold that thought." Then he winked at me. "Boy, give this woman a slice of pie and she's putty in my hands."

I laughed and thought about the wild romantic plans we had made when we first got married. The reality of six children had, shall we say, adjusted those plans a wee bit. Even though we couldn't be as spontaneous as we were before parenthood, there was greater love, and even passion, if we could ever schedule in an intimate interlude.

"Trains crashing in the night," I mumbled as we fell into bed a few hours later. The children were all finally asleep, and it felt heavenly to lie down next to Brian and relax. I thought about how different my life was, raising Erica and five boys.

"You men are so . . . strange," I said.

"Excuse me? I'm a plural now?"

I stared at the ceiling. "You're all so . . . so . . . odd."

"What now?" Brian abandoned his plan to get right to sleep.

"Well, you have this inefficient vocabulary—hair but no bangs, shirts but no tops . . . the boys even call their underwear 'shorts.'"

"What is your point?"

"Why do you always ask me what my point is?" I said, pretending to be indignant. "What is this fixation you have with points?"

Brian smiled. "You don't have one, do you?"

"I most certainly do," I said, groping frantically for a good one. "My point is this. You men types aren't specific enough. Shorts could mean anything—cut-offs, tennis shorts—"

"And what do you call them?"

"Panties, of course," I said. "You say panties and everybody knows exactly what you're talking about. You say shorts, and it might not mean underwear at all."

"You're right," Brian said, scooting away and eyeing me as if I'd lost my mind. "Men are the strange ones."

I laughed and pulled him back over to me.

"Hey," Brian said, "it's lucky I set the kids straight. Otherwise, our boys would be running around in panties, tops and bangs. Now that matter is settled, so let's go to sleep."

I turned to him, exhausted but completely unable to sleep. "Just because you sleep in a king-size bed doesn't make you a king, you know."

"Sleep? Who gets any sleep anymore?"

I sighed. "I'm sorry. I'm just so exhausted I can't relax."

"Here," Brian said, flicking his bedside radio on. "I'll set the timer and you can listen to some music."

Perfect, I thought. Some soft, soothing music would be just what I needed.

We listened as a woman's voice sang softly into the night. "Sounds like Pia Zadora," I said. "Whatever happened to her, anyway?"

Brian sighed. "I think one night her husband was trying to sleep and she wanted to talk. So he shot her. I'm not sure. Maybe he strangled her."

Now I was twisting my lips in an effort not to laugh and thus encourage Brian in his ludicrous story.

"I'm not sure," he continued. "He told the jury how she always talked when he was trying to sleep, and they let him off. Justifiable homicide."

"You're not funny," I said, trying to sound serious.

Suddenly a crackly woman's voice was screeching, then singing, "I Feel Good," that old James Brown song from the sixties.

Brian and I stared at each other. "Is that who I think it is?" Brian whispered. I nodded, speechless.

"That's 'I Feel Good' with Edith Horvitz," the disc jockey said. "And for all you Edith Horvitz fans, this week's Billboard Magazine says her song is number two with a bullet!"

CHAPTER 9

MEDALS AND STARS

Brian and I both sat bolt upright in bed, neither of us able to speak for a few seconds.

"How can that possibly be a hit song?" Brian finally whispered.

I shook my head. "Maybe it's one of those gag songs," I said.

"You could gag, all right," Brian muttered.

"I mean, popular for being funny. Like 'Monster Mash' and 'Disco Duck' were."

Brian was still stunned, and lay back down. "That woman is incredible."

I fluffed my pillow and settled back with Brian. "Hey—maybe she'll go on tour. Be on Jay Leno. Dine with the president."

Brian sighed. "And to think all this began when you asked her to be the homemaking director."

I shrugged. "Join the Relief Society and see the world."

The next morning I had to call Edith and congratulate her.

"Well, it's a real honor," she said.

"Brian and I heard it on the radio last night," I continued. "Number two with a bullet—wow!"

"Oh—you're talking about my song!" Edith laughed. "Yeah, I can't wait to get back over to England and do my seventies tape."

"You're doing a tape for the First Quorum of the Seventies?" I asked.

"Andy," Edith said, the same patronizing way I've said 'Edith' to her a zillion times, "Of course not. It's music from the 1970s."

I was so embarrassed not to have realized what she meant. Was I losing my mind as Edith was gaining sanity? Were Edith and I trading places?

"Oh, the seventies—of course," I murmured.

"I can't wait to get to the nineties," Edith said. "I want to do 'Achy Breaky Heart' and some rap stuff."

With the London Philharmonic? I could just picture it. "Edith," I said, "What did you think I was calling about when you said it was a real honor?"

"Oh," Edith said, sounding modest for the first time since I've known her. "I thought you meant that Nobel thing."

"What Nobel thing?"

"The article in the paper this morning," she said.

I dragged the phone cord into the dining room where the paper had been left in a shambles after Grayson had clipped it to shreds for current events articles to take to school. "Hang on," I said, finally turning the front section over. There, on the lower half of the front page was the headline, "Local Woman Wins Nobel Prize."

As I began to read and my mouth dropped open, I heard Edith faintly in my ear, saying, "I've got that call waiting thing, Andy. I'll call you back." And she hung up.

My knees turned to jelly as I slumped into a chair and read. Edith had won the Nobel prize for chemistry! Her glue had some kind of revolutionary molecular structure that approximated skin itself, and was being used by surgeons around the world. They were grafting with it, healing wounds with it, and using it in place of stitches. Never before had medical science seen anything like it, and it was being hailed as the invention of the century.

"Brian, have you read the paper?" I asked, catching him at his office at the university.

"Just glanced at the front page," he said. "Why?"

"Glance again. Edith Horvitz has won the Nobel prize for that crazy glue of hers. It has revolutionized surgical procedures, something about the space program . . ."

"Andy," Brian said, "you can fool some of the people all of the time, and all of the people some of the time, but me—never."

"Well, read it for yourself," I said.

I could hear papers rattling over the phone. "Holy cow," Brian said. "I didn't even know she had been nominated. And we thought she was just a run-of-the-mill rock star."

The article mentioned Edith's hit song, her adventures in rescuing Nick in England, her "ongoing friendship" with the queen of England, and even the house that she built from particle board and hot glue. Then it compared her to Ben Franklin and Leonardo da Vinci (my Ninja Turtle fan children would be pleased), because her achievements were so diverse. One of the judges even called her a "Renaissance woman."

"I used to dream I was famous when I was a little girl," Edith was quoted as saying. "I guess it's just my dream coming true."

Maybe she was right, and fame was Edith's destiny. I certainly remembered our first meeting, when a TV news crew was interviewing her, then again when the media ran her picture capturing the terrorists in England.

I called Edith back and insisted we throw a big party to celebrate the award. "Hot dog," she exclaimed. "I'll be there!" And to think she called it "that Nobel thing."

"It really isn't any big deal," Edith said at the party. "I've always liked dabbling in chemistry. Chemistry and crochet, of course." Edith was priceless.

Naturally, Nick's pharmaceutical company was thrilled; they owned the patent and were raking in a fortune. And Edith, sitting on a crocheted nest of millions, did indeed make the publicity rounds, appearing on talk shows and being interviewed by reporters. She always put in a plug for her hit song, which kept it steady on the charts. No one suspected that Edith was a little nuts; everyone saw her as an eccentric—a goofy-looking scientist in a yellow housecoat, dangly earrings and maroon lipstick. She was quirky and outspoken, the perfect character to interview.

Within a month, Edith was approached by a Hollywood studio about making a movie of her life. She dragged me with her to the interview, claiming I was an integral part of the story, and ought to be there to help "check out these guys."

We drove past the guard booth onto the lot, followed an intricate path to a parking space, then met the producers in a glass-and-chrome office that overlooked the city. After formal introductions and a dozen refused offers of cappuccino, cafe ole, cafe mocha, espresso macchiato and cafe latte, a guy in Italian shoes and a wild tie said, "So Edith, how do you see your life?"

"I see it in one of those Omnimax theaters," Edith said, her eyes twinkling. "With fifty cameras . . . you know, like they have at world's fairs."

The men exchanged chuckles. "Seriously," Wild Tie went on. "Give us a capsule."

"A capsule of what?"

"Of your life!" The Hollywood set had the same unspoken "duh" at the ends of their sentences that my children had.

"Well, it started out kinda boring," Edith said. "I was orphaned and raised by my aunt. But . . ." then she grinned. "I guess I have one of those late-bloomer stories, 'cause life sure got exciting, huh?" Then she gave them the brief summary we'd practiced in the car on the way over.

"We love the orphan angle, and the spy rescue concept is a killer," another fellow said, this one wearing a blazer over a T-shirt with a picture of the Planet Earth on the front.

"Love the rescue," a third man echoed. He kept nodding like those big-headed dolls people used to put in their back car windows.

"Obviously, we want the hit song and the Nobel prize," Planet Earth said.

"Nobel prize is great," Wild Tie agreed.

"But let's lose the particle board house and the crocheting." Planet Earth scowled and the others copied him.

"No good," the others murmured. "The house has to go."

Obviously, Planet Earth called the shots. I stared, marveling at these people who were slicing up Edith's life and tossing the less cinematic parts aside.

"The mental hospital could work," Planet Earth continued. "The suffering, the pathos of being locked up unjustly—without making you a victim, of course."

"No victims," Big Head smiled, wagging a finger. "Victims are unsympathetic."

"But the queen of England . . ." Planet Earth went on, twisting his mouth as he considered whether to ax the reigning British monarch or not. "Nah. Who is she, anyway? I mean, really, who is she?"

Wild Tie shrugged. "Exactly. Who is she?"

"She's the queen of England," I said, speaking up at last.

Planet Earth wrinkled his nose. "Queens are passé. What do they do—hunt foxes? P. I."

"P. I.?" I asked.

"Politically incorrect," Big Head said. But of course.

Edith had been listening to all this with a confused expression on her face. Finally she said, "So do you want to make a movie of my life or what?"

"Edith," Planet Earth said, as if he were falling in love with her on the spot, "We love your life. Your life is . . . *our* life. Guys?"

The other two nodded, suddenly bubbling with enthusiasm. "Your life is fantastic," Big Head said. "We love it."

"Absolutely," Wild Tie agreed. "You sure you two wouldn't like some cappuccino? Cafe ole? We have cinnamon and nutmeg."

By the time the meeting ended, I felt I had already seen a movie of Edith's life—the asylum part.

"Well, that was interesting," I said to Edith as we got in the car.

"Ha!" she scoffed. "Are you kidding? That was nuts. If those guys aren't on drugs, they should be. And I know just the medication."

I chuckled. For all her shock therapy and missing links, Edith seemed to have retained the most important ones. She had the remarkable, childlike skill of sizing up strangers in an instant, and she pulled no punches in sharing her discoveries. "How'd you like that one in the T-shirt?" Edith said. "Save the planet, but go through twenty Styrofoam cups in an hour."

"He seemed to be the one in charge."

"Yeah," Edith said. "Just like this woman I knew in the

hospital—Bunny something. You name a kid Bunny, I guarantee she'll end up in therapy. Anyway, she had this little gang of followers and whatever she said, they'd repeat it. She could've said, 'Walk on the ceiling,' and they would've tried it."

"Well, those guys seem serious about turning your life into a movie," I said.

"But they don't want my particle board house," Edith reminded me, as if this could be the deal-breaker.

"Maybe they're just afraid they can't duplicate it," I said.

Edith smiled. "I never thought of that. You're probably right. Well, I'll call them and say okay after I get back from the library. I gotta return some overdue books."

I glanced over at Edith and smiled. From receiving a teapot from the queen of England to selling her life's story to Hollywood, nothing budged Edith from putting first things first. And in this case, that meant lugging a book on chemistry and pest control back to the library, with 35 cents in late fees.

The next morning my phone rang, and when I picked it up, Edith's voice snapped, "Deal's off."

"Is this Edith?" I asked. "What deal are you talking about?"

"The movie deal. I just got off the phone with those guys. We were right. They're nuts."

"What happened?"

"I told 'em I only got one life, right? Correct me if I'm wrong, Andy."

"No, one is it, Edith."

"Okay." She was laying it out as logically as possible. "So if a movie is gonna be made about me, I want my say-so in what actress gets to play me. That's only fair, right?"

"Umm . . ."

"So I asked for Meryl Streep."

"Uh . . . okay." I pulled up a chair for the rest of the story.

"They said no. Actually they said no in Spanish. *No possible*. These guys speak about as much Spanish as my crocheted poodle. So I answered them in Pig Latin."

"You what?"

"Why not? Long as we're not sticking with English, I figure the world is my lobster."

"You mean oyster?"

"Oyster, lobster, whatever," Edith said, anxious to continue her story. "So I said, en-thay I-yay ant-way—"

"Edith," I said, aware that she was rather worked up, and trying to interrupt her as gently as possible, "can you tell me in English?"

"You I'll tell," she conceded. "So I said Michelle Pfeiffer, then."

"You wanted Michelle Pfeiffer to play you in a movie?" I tried to conceal my astonishment.

"You got it," Edith said. "Can you believe they refused? I could see I'd have nothing but headaches working with those clowns. So I fired them."

"But you hadn't exactly hired them," I said.

"Fired 'em anyway," Edith said, obviously exhilarated by her shrewd business skills. I could picture her with a sword and eye patch, standing on the bow of a pirate ship and commanding the cannons to be "fired anyway."

I sighed. "Sounds like you're happy with your decision."

"Yeah," Edith said. I could almost see one eyebrow raise as she added, "They didn't want my particle board house, remember."

"I remember."

Edith snickered. "Guess I showed them."

"You drive a hard bargain," I agreed. Edith could win a Nobel prize for unyielding standards, hands down.

CHAPTER 10

THE MOTHERS OF INVENTIONS

Edith immediately launched Edith Enterprises (EE) and began cranking out more inventions. "Some o' these I thought up a long time ago," she confessed to me one day, "and maybe now folks'll listen to me."

A visit to her home was mind-boggling. Patent applications, articles she was working on, and scholarly journals were stacked on every available (and still crocheted) surface. Her kitchen, which had always had pots of curious ingredients simmering on the stove, was now a full-blown laboratory, complete with test tubes and beakers. And Edith, more often than not, answered her door wearing an apron and goggles to protect her from who-knows-what chemicals.

"Come on in," she called as I tapped on her screen door one day. The triplets were now three, and had just started a preschool class two mornings a week. It seemed ages since I had dropped in on Edith, so I popped over at the first opportunity.

"I'm working on shampoos," Edith said, waving to the sofa as if there were anywhere to sit on it. "Don't you think adult shampoos ought to be tearless, too?"

"Hmm?" I leaned against the arm of a chair.

"Like kids' shampoos," Edith continued. "I mean, what's the matter with these companies? Do they think it doesn't sting once you're an adult? Don't these pinheads ever get soap in *their* eyes?"

I nodded. "Yeah," I said, rallying around her cause. "If they can make it for children, why not for the rest of us?"

Edith waved a prong-looking thing at me. "What's next—"
she sneered, "Lamaze breathing classes to teach adults how
to deal with the pain of getting shampoo in their eyes? And to
think we stand there in the shower, like dopes, letting them
put one over on us." Edith lifted something stringy out of a pot,
using the prong instrument. "It's another conspiracy," she
said, as if this were perfectly obvious. "Tell you what else I'm
going to market," she said. "Scented key rings."

Well, she had already catapulted her scented earrings from
a homemaking night class into a legitimate jewelry item, so
why not key rings as well? Scented jewelry was the latest
rage, although Edith had reluctantly changed the fragrances
to popular perfume scents instead of pine trees and bananas.

"I love smells," Edith said. "I figure this is gonna be a life-
saver for folks who can't find their keys. Just follow your nose!
I figure cinnamon, garlic, maybe a cheese scent. What do you
think?"

"Gee," I said, imagining my car reeking of Gorgonzola, "I
think you'd better use perfumes again. People's purses and cars
will have the smell of the key rings," I said.

"Yeah. So?"

"Well, not everyone likes a constant smell of garlic and
cheese," I tried to explain.

Edith laughed. "Are you kidding? People smell garlic bread
and go *crazy!* I know I do."

Well, I couldn't argue with her there.

"I got another plan for Edith Enterprises," she said. "Still
wish I woulda called it Edith *Sur*prises. Oh, well." She poured
the entire pot of goop into another tub, then dumped in a bottle of green powder. "Airport llamas," she said.

"What!"

"This one came to me like a hernia, striking me right in the
groin as I was lifting my luggage off the carousel," she said.
"Sky caps never go into the parking lot with you, and those fold-
up things always snap like bear traps when *I* use 'em."

I listened, my jaw hanging.

"So," Edith went on, "Why not foster friendly relations
with Chile and Peru, and import a few hundred llamas to

schlepp baggage at the airport? So they spit a little. You tell the tourists it's raining."

"But—"

"I know what you're thinking," Edith said, proud of having remained one step ahead. "They only go in one spot, so it's almost like they're house broken. I checked."

I tried to imagine that phone call. "What about the sky caps' unions?" I asked.

Edith shrugged. "Hey. If half the workers in the country can be replaced by computers and robots, then those guys can easily be replaced by a few llamas."

I just stared. A month ago, Edith had been the speaker at a dermatologist's convention where she had actually implored them to explore the principles of hydroseeding in restoring hair to bald heads. She had even volunteered herself as a guinea pig. "Please," she had said, with a laugh. "Look. We can put men on the moon—heck, we could probably get *hair* to grow on the moon, but we can't get it to grow out of bald heads. I say we spray new follicles into the scalp. They shoot novocaine into your gums, why not seedlings into your head?"

Next she addressed a convention of facialists, outlining her software idea for a computer that she called her "Automatic Aging Machine." ("And it's not a tanning booth," Brian had quipped as he read about it in the paper.) Her idea was to photograph the customer, then have her watch as her face got old and wrinkled on TV, right before her eyes. The jowls would sag, the eyes would droop. "I guarantee this will throw fear and panic into everybody who sees it," she promised. "One look at themselves at ninety, and they'll buy any product you want to sell them."

"Been thinking about another jewelry line," Edith said, letting her concoction simmer and wiping her hands on a white towel. "Looked into bug sprays, pest control, all that stuff. Do you have any idea how much people spend to keep mosquitoes off 'em? So I figure we could market bug-repellent jewelry."

I smiled. As one who gets eaten alive just stepping outside to pick up the mail, I had to admit I'd give it a try.

"Who likes to spray that greasy, stinky stuff all over their arms and legs?" Edith said, right on the heels of suggesting garlic-scented key rings. "Plus it gets all over your clothes."

"True," I said.

"So you wear a Bug-Away Bracelet, or a No-Pest Necklace and bingo! You're home free. I think a lot of single ladies will wear the No-Pest Necklace as a Levitical statement, too."

"You mean a political statement?"

"That's what I said. You know, as a joke to keep certain men away."

I laughed. She was probably right. Edith moved a stack of notebooks off a chair and sat down, tired from her morning's work. "These are worth more than anything in the house," Edith said, carefully placing the notebooks in front of a full bookcase. "They're all my failures, all the stuff that didn't work."

"Your failures are the most valuable thing you own?"

Edith smiled. "Andy, everybody's are. How come I'm the only person who's figured that out? How do people think I won the Nobel prize, anyway—by accident?" She chortled as I realized that, yes, the thought had actually occurred to me. Edith leaned in to instruct me. "How many experiments did Edison do before he finally got the light bulb right?"

"Hundreds?" I guessed.

"Thousands. And if you don't keep track of what doesn't work, how do you keep from repeating it? That's supposed to be the difference between humans and animals—we can pass on what we've learned through our experiences."

Good heavens. Had Edith been this smart when I first met her?

Just then a buzzer went off, and Edith went back into the kitchen. "That's my dehydrator; I'm making Angel some lunch."

That macaw was still living like a king, leering at guests and making his usual unprintable comments.

I could hear Edith laughing in the kitchen. "He did it again!" she said, coming out and wagging a finger at her naughty parrot. Then she turned to me. "Did you know that a macaw can mimic microwave ovens, disposals, you-name-it?"

I forced a smile, recalling my own similar adventures with that bird.

"When he gets hungry he buzzes like my dehydrator so I'll get up and feed him," Edith said. "Smart bird, huh?" She poured something from a paper bag into his cage, which sounded like gravel as it filled his bowl. "I eat this myself," she said. That wasn't surprising. "How are the triplets?" she asked.

"Oh, wonderful," I said. This was one of the rare times when not one of them had a cold or other problem. The zombie period was over, and now it was simply a matter of raising six children. We were still doing laundry in an assembly line and buying food in sizes that looked like something Fred Flintstone would purchase, but life was no more chaotic than other big families were experiencing.

"I thought you were gonna collapse those first couple of years," Edith said. "But I guess you turned the hump." Did she mean I turned the corner? Or that I was over the hump?

"I nearly invented some special handcuffs for you to put on those kids," she added. I couldn't help thinking that every mother in the world would buy them. "Did you give them vitamins when they were babies?"

"Gosh, Edith, maybe you've hit on something here. Maybe we gave them too many vitamins. Maybe that's why they were so wired."

Edith laughed. "Nah. You probably gave them the right amount. Face it, Andy, you had three boys all the same age. *You* were the one who needed vitamins. Anyway, lots of folks don't give their babies vitamins. Especially your poor folks. So I figure we can raise a generation of healthier kids if we implant some kind of time-released vitamin into the handles of shopping carts."

"Excuse me?"

Edith chuckled. "That's what I like about you, Andy. You always admit it when you don't understand something." This was a compliment? Edith continued. "You'd be surprised how many people I talk to—and I *know* they have no idea what I'm talking about—who nod and rub their chins and say, 'Uh-huh, Uh-huh.'" Edith was a riot mimicking the frowning pseudo-intellectuals who suddenly filled her world. "But not you," she went on. "No sir! If Andy doesn't get it, Andy tells you. If it's over Andy's head—"

"I get your point," I interrupted. "You were saying about shopping cart handles?"

"Oh—right. Well, even poor folks go to the grocery store. And every baby, rich or poor, gums the handles. Moms stop them, but they go right back to it. What if, instead of passing germs, it made kids healthier? Maybe the parents could even absorb it through their hands!"

I sighed. "Well, that's a thought, Edith." Where did she get this stuff?

"Also, I was thinking about Erica," Edith said. "She's fourteen now, right?"

"Rumor has it." It was still hard for me to believe that my baby girl was only two years away from dating. And Grayson was a deacon who was growing so fast that his pants always looked an inch too short. Ryan was nine, still bouncing off the walls and making his teachers (and his parents) gray before their time.

"Well, how is that?" Edith asked.

"Having a teenager?" I smiled. "It's everything you've heard and more."

Edith threw her head back and laughed. "She's a good kid, though. I can tell."

That was true. Erica was a relentless student, almost too demanding of herself. Unfortunately, she enjoyed holding her mother up to the same impossible standards she had for herself. It left us both miserably lacking and extremely frustrated. Erica was convinced she'd been stolen at birth by a woman far inferior to other moms. This woman, this thief—me—was a source of continual embarrassment, a woman so hopelessly out of it that Erica's only option for survival was to keep as much distance between us as possible, particularly in public. At least, these were the results of the latest poll.

"Well, I've got the answer," Edith said. "Not for Erica, really. She'll be okay. But for the teenagers who think they know everything. You know, the ones who drive their parents crazy. It's called 'Run-the-World Camp.'" She opened a notebook to quote from her proposal.

I smiled. "Tell me about it. I may want to invest."

"It would be like Disneyland," Edith said, "only based on the earth's countries. Kids would spend a week or two solving international and domestic problems. They would be assigned computer offspring who would appear on their screens and whine about staying out late, wearing stupid-looking clothes, and in general, deliver sassy comments."

"So far, so good," I said.

"Then, on a keyboard," Edith explained, "teenagers would have to make moral, ethical, economic and social decisions. Wrong answers would blow up various sections of the park."

I laughed. "Every parent would sign their kids up."

"Darn right they would. Maybe even permanently."

I laughed. "Let's hope Erica won't blow up any nations."

Edith shrugged. "At least any that are friendly to ours."

"What's this?" I asked, picking up the top document on a stack of papers in the chair.

"Oh, that's my fiber optics outline. You wouldn't understand it."

Immediately I began scanning it to prove her wrong. I must have read the same paragraph three times before I looked up and said, "Well, it's a long document. Maybe you could summarize it for me."

Edith winked. "It's about using fiber optics in the back windshields of cars, to send messages to other cars. Just for fun, really. People could apologize for cutting you off—but probably no one would. Or they could say thank you, or invite someone to dinner. Mainly I thought folks could express their opinions with it, instead of gumming up their cars with all those bumper stickers."

"Edith, you need your own TV show," I said. "Miss Wizard."

"Who has the time? Soon as I finish with this shampoo idea, I'm getting right to work on a special paint idea."

I propped my chin up on my elbow, leaning over a table to listen.

"This paint would be better than a lie detector."

"Huh?"

"I've isolated some molecules that I think can be mixed into latex paint," she said, "and have the same effect as mood rings, only all over the walls!" Edith's eyes were twinkling at the possibilities. "I got the idea from that mood ring I picked up in England when I exchanged the queen's teapot."

"Yes, I remember that."

"I thought, why not change the colors of your room as your mood changes? Plus, it could almost be like mind reading. Picture a boss interviewing a salesman, let's say, and being able to tell from his walls if the guy had the confidence for sales! Teachers would know if their students were bored or if they understood her; you and Brian would know how each other felt; even the President would know how his advisors felt about something—just by glancing at a wall!"

"But . . . what color is the paint?" I asked.

"Right now, it's like a mood ring," Edith said. "Kind of dark, swirly purples and greens. That's what I gotta work on. Getting it to mix with white paint."

"What if people don't want others to know what they're thinking?" I asked.

Edith smirked. "Well, that's just too bad, isn't it? This is gonna launch America into a whole new level of honesty."

I could only imagine the sparks that would fly at Camp David if a world leader made the President's walls turn black.

"I can see several possibilities," I said.

"Wait 'til interior desecraters get hold of this," she said.

"You mean decorators?"

Edith sighed. "Andy, you keep repeating the stuff I say. Have you ever considered getting your hearing checked?"

I smiled. Yet another of Edith's brilliant ideas.

DESPERATION AND INSPIRATION

Not every family resorts to the Terrorism School of Parenting, but Brian thought he'd give it a try. After all, none of the experts' methods seemed to work on our brood.

"And brood is the right word for it," Brian had said.

I had to admit, I knew we needed an unorthodox idea (but not as unorthodox as Edith's ideas) when I said to three-year-old Cameron, "I'll bet I can win the race up to your bedroom" to get him to take a nap, and he laughed right in my face, "Go ahead."

"These triplets don't fall for the same things the older three did," I complained to Brian one night.

"That's because they have a think tank," Brian said. "I've seen it. They huddle under a card table and compare notes. Then they vote on what's a ploy that we're using, and what's for real."

I almost believed him. Even as babies when I had tried to zoom a spoonful of squash into their mouths, complete with airplane sound effects, they had stared at me like I was bonkers (any fool could see it was a spoon of squash, not an airplane).

And recently, when I read them the story of Little Red Riding Hood, Austin immediately asked, "Why didn't the wolf just eat her up when he first saw her?"

Indeed. Why would dressing up as a grandma facilitate his hunting skills?

"I guess he didn't think of that," I said.

"But he thought of hiding at her grandma's?" Austin had no patience with illogical story lines.

"He could have eaten her up and then still gone and eaten up the grandma," Cameron agreed.

"*And* the basket of goodies," Austin nodded.

Bennett shrugged. "Also, wolves can't talk."

I felt like I was reading fairy tales to a panel of literary critics.

Another time I was singing them to sleep (or so I thought), when I launched into a verse of "Row, Row, Row Your Boat." Just as I came to "Life is but a dream," Austin said, "Some song. What does that mean—if you wake up you're dead?"

The other two began squealing and giggling, Cameron sitting up with his eyes open, saying, "Dead," then falling back onto his pillow with them shut, saying, "Alive."

And only the previous evening, they had launched into an in-depth discussion of the origins of Jell-O during dinner.

"Gelatin comes from cow's knees," Austin had announced, his mouth full of Exhibit A.

"That's right," Grayson had said, pleased that his tutelage was paying off.

"And they get the grease out with acid," Cameron chimed in.

"And," Bennett said, raising a chubby finger to punctuate his topper, "they grow bacteria in it!"

Brian had watched me writhe and grinned. "Bon appetit," he said, raising a spoonful of Jell-O into the air.

"Bone is right," Eric had said, poking the jiggly mass on her salad plate. Naturally the triplets had launched into hysterics at this point, and Brian had shrugged with mixed innocence and self-satisfaction.

"I have an idea how to get the kids to clean up their rooms," Brian said, breaking into my reverie. "I'm going to gather up all their stuff that's strewn around, then sell it back to them."

"That sounds like kidnapping," I said.

"Toy napping," Brian corrected. "And anyway, it's more like extortion than kidnapping."

"Oh!" I said, pretending this was a great relief. "Well, then."

"Hey," Brian said, "desperate times call for desperate measures."

I shrugged. It couldn't be less successful than our other attempts.

The following day, Brian scooped up what seemed like tons of underwear, shirts (not tops, thank you), socks, toys, magazines, rocks and game pieces, and put them into three large boxes.

Ryan came home to find the following note pinned to his door:

"Your favorite teddy bear is being held hostage in a secret location. The price for his return is to free some prisoners from squalor, namely your family. If this room is not spotless and clean by one week from today, the teddy bear dies. His execution will be at dawn Wednesday morning."

"Where's my bear?" Ryan yelled, echoing downstairs. "Give me back my bear!!"

Brian met him on the stairway. "Only if you meet the terms of the bear nappers."

Ryan folded his arms. "Then I'm calling the police."

Brian made room for Ryan to pass by, with a sweeping wave of his arm. "Be my guest."

Ryan's eyes narrowed into slits. "I want my bear back."

Despite being almost ten, Ryan cherished a particular fluorescent teddy bear that wore sunglasses and a surfer shirt.

"Clean your room, then," Erica said, marching past Ryan to her own room. Within seconds we heard an ear-piercing scream. Erica flew down the stairs and into the family room. "This is, like, totally unconstitutional," Erica said. "Life around here is so unfair. Where is all my stuff?"

"I'm glad you asked," Brian said, leading his pouty children to three big boxes in the living room. "Welcome to the Taylor General Store. After dinner, the store will open to sell goods and commodities of all kinds. Games, books, puzzles, clothing," then he leaned into Erica's face, "necklaces."

"This is really low, Dad," Grayson said, appearing on the scene with Cameron and Austin. "How are the triplets going to clean their room? They're only three."

"Triplets get an age exemption," Brian said.

Now Grayson was even more indignant. "No fair!"

Sure enough, once dinner was through, we depleted the kids' savings as they purchased some of the trinkets they couldn't live without. Ryan, distracted by the task of sawing an old baseball in two, had forgotten what treasures he was still missing. Grayson was grumbling and complaining, even blaming me for the idea because I was hanging around so much with Sister Horvitz. Erica was furious and had stormed off to her room, refusing to speak to either of us.

The triplets were the only happy ones, particularly once they learned that they might get to witness the beheading of Ryan's teddy bear.

Brian and I surveyed the boxes of junk, which looked just as full as ever.

"Maybe we should have lowered our prices," I said. "We still have a lot of inventory."

Brian sighed. "Yeah. I feel so mean."

We just stared at the boxes, then up towards our unhappy children.

"But, they have to learn somehow," I said. "Right?"

The next day we scoured the bookstore for a parenting book we didn't own (a tough conquest in the Taylor family), which we hoped would contain a chapter on how to make neatniks out of slobs.

For fifteen minutes we pored over the offerings, finding little to help us. Brian sighed. "We're getting no place," he said.

"All these books are about babies," I mumbled, scanning the spines of a row of books. "Oh—now we're getting older."

"We certainly are," Brian deadpanned.

I pinched his ribs. "Come on. We'll find something."

"How old is your child?" a clerk asked.

"Three," Brian said. "Squared."

"We have triplets," I explained to the puzzled clerk. His eyes grew round. "And . . . some others," I said.

The clerk sighed and shook his head. "Good luck!" Then he noticed the Sorbonne University sweatshirt I was wearing, one I'd bought in Paris when we were there with Nick and Zan. "Oh—you went to the Sorbonne?" the clerk asked.

"No," I admitted. "I just bought it when I was in France."

"Oh." The clerk frowned as if I were a sandbagger trying to pass myself off as a Sorbonne graduate.

Brian and I left empty-handed. That Monday I thought I would teach another family home evening lesson on keeping a clean and orderly house. Perhaps this time, I thought, it would sink in.

But on Monday afternoon, as I was studying my scriptures (where I should have looked for ideas in the first place), I got a burst of inspiration and changed the topic entirely. Like so many answers to my prayers, it had nothing to do with the scripture I was actually reading. But the *act* of reading had cleared my channel, so to speak, and I was able to hear the revelation I needed for my children. I shared my idea with Brian and he agreed to try it.

"Tonight's lesson is on generosity," I said. "And the Church's welfare program." I then told the children how important it was for us to take care of those less fortunate, and that I had an easy way for them to get involved. "Dad and I are giving you back all your toys."

The kids leaped from their chairs, cheering.

"And teddy gets a stay of execution," Brian announced as he tossed the bear to a beaming Ryan.

"So," I said, as they suddenly fell silent again, "from now on you'll have the chance to help others. Anything you'd like to give to the needy, just leave on the floor and I'll pick it up each morning." I then hung an ominous black trash bag on their doorknobs as a reminder.

The kids sat there in a stupor of shock. It was wonderful.

After the lesson, you have never seen twelve little legs and hands move so fast to put away toys and clothing.

That night, after countless kisses of congratulations from my admiring husband, I tiptoed down the hall to check on the sleeping kids. Erica's room almost sparkled in the moonlight. The triplets dozed in three little beds, their floor offering no clue that three rambunctious boys lived here. Grayson's room was nearly as sterile as an operating room, every hint of a belonging put carefully away.

I opened Ryan's door. There he snoozed in what used to be the messiest room in the house (and maybe on the planet). But now, his treasures were stuffed into drawers and cubbyholes. It still needed organizing, but at least the floor was spotless. As I turned to leave, I noticed one object in the shadows near the foot of his bed which hadn't been put away. Bending down, I saw that Ryan had left his teddy bear on the floor. I knew Ryan's heart would break to lose the bear, so I picked it up to secretly place it on a shelf. Then I noticed that a scrap of paper was taped to its chest. Walking out into the hall where I could turn on a light, I read, "To whoever gets this bear I hope you like him. He is very speshul."

12

MOM-O'-WAR

Natalie, my little sister who should make commercials for the singles' program, vows she will never have children. "I mean, look at you," she said, waving at the laundry I was carrying upstairs when she dropped by one afternoon. As if one load of laundry defined the entire motherhood experience.

"Also, my mind would turn to mush," she says. "I need adventure and mental stimulation."

I put the laundry basket down and felt her forehead. "I didn't know your mind was at risk," I said. This wasn't exactly true; Natalie has been at mush risk since childhood.

"Ha ha," Natalie yawned. "Face it; how stimulating can it be to pack lunches and change bedding all day?"

I chuckled and shook my head. "There's a tiny bit more to it than that," I said. "Besides, a bright mind is bright wherever you put it. It doesn't matter if it's a church calling or a profession or parenting. If you're lazy or whiny by nature, you'll take that attitude into whatever job you're doing. But if you're creative, energetic, and goal-oriented, then that's the kind of mom you are, too. It's only boring to boring people."

"But . . ." Natalie shuddered. "Kids!"

I love a smug expression, particularly if it's on my face, and there was one there now. "Natalie, not to change the subject, but I'm doing some research and I need your help. I mean, since you're out there in the world of single adult thought and all."

Natalie smiled, eager to share her vast wisdom.

"Do you know if sea horses can bite?"

Natalie shrugged. "Beats me."

"Or if elephants snore?"

"Why do you need to know this animal stuff?" Natalie asked, sitting down to watch me fold the laundry.

"Oh, it isn't just animal stuff," I said. "I also need the history of the alphabet. If there are capital letters and small letters, why aren't there any middle-sized letters?"

Natalie smiled. "I never thought of that. And . . . I don't know."

"If a seaplane lands on water," I went on, "how do the people get out? Also, why do owls come out at night? And if it's to eat mice, then why do mice come out at night? Also, do bees like music? And why don't bugs like yellow lights? Do germs communicate with one another? And if so, how? Do you think koala bears like honey? And when is God's birthday?"

Natalie just stared at me.

I continued. "Why do people eat out at restaurants that are decorated to look like cozy homes when they could just stay home in the first place? What makes spider webs sticky? How does an antennae change channels? What are jeepers and creepers? How high is the sky? And what keeps the planets up?"

Natalie shook her head. "Good grief, Andy—how many college degrees do you think I have? I think you'd better call Sister Horvitz—she's the one who won the Nobel prize for that sort of thing."

"I guess it would take a Nobel prize winner to answer those," I mused. "But she travels a lot, so I can't always call her when the kids ask me these things."

Natalie sat there, silent. "Okay," she said. "So motherhood is more intellectual than I thought. But it's still a thankless job."

I smiled. "No it isn't. I feel appreciated all the time. Last week Cameron was riding in the car with me, and the sun was shining in his eyes. He said, 'Mommy, could you please move the sun?' That kid thinks I can do anything!"

Natalie chuckled.

"And yesterday Austin woke me up saying, 'I love your face so much I feel all tickly. Can I smell your neck? Will your cheeks always be so soft? When I grow up and marry you, I'm going to give you a whole list of cars.'"

"A *list?*" Natalie laughed. "Gee, what a guy."

"One time Bennett said, 'I love you so much I could just squeeze your whole, skinny hand off.'"

Natalie listened, then softly said, "It's like you're their whole world."

I looked up from the laundry and smiled. "Yeah."

"Okay, but don't tell me that kids don't make you feel exhausted."

"Oh, they do," I said, drifting off to other happy memories. "It's . . . great."

Natalie stared at me, then shook her head. "You're weird, Andy." Natalie was semiactive, and among the gospel principles that she chose to view as an optional smorgasbord item was the divine role of motherhood.

I sighed and returned to the present. "So what did you want to borrow? I mean—what brings you over?" I blushed.

Natalie smirked. "I don't just come over when I need to borrow something, you know." We went back downstairs. "Sometimes I come by just to say hello."

"Well, how nice," I said.

"Oh—I just thought of something," she said, her hand on the doorknob to leave. "You guys have a set of those big party bowls, don't you? I totally forgot! Wow! And I'm bringing a salad to this big picnic next week at work. You wouldn't mind if I took one, would you?" Natalie is a terrible actress.

I led her into the kitchen and pulled one out of the cupboard for her. "Thanks," she called as she skipped down the front walk. "I'll bring it back next week!" I knew it would be a month.

In a few days we had Nick and Zan over for dinner. Afterwards, Brian was helping me with the dishes while Nick and Zan were in the back yard watching the blur of little bodies running by. "The kids ask such amazing questions," I said to him, reflecting on Natalie's visit.

"Kids are curious," Brian said. "Zan says Nolan asks the same kinds of questions to her."

"Yes, but Zan can answer them." She and Nick had also had another baby a year ago, a darling baby girl they named Blair. And by all counts, Blair was even brighter than Nolan, who was already reading at barely three years old.

"Blair will probably read the directions to the crib and

then disassemble it before she'll climb out of it," Brian said. "And Nolan is probably asking about mutual funds, not sea horses." Indeed, Nick and Zan had evidently given birth to two kids who were forever going to throw off the bell curve. These children seemed absolutely perfect. Blair didn't even need a bib to eat!

"How do you keep up?" Zan asked, coming in from outside. "I'm glad Nolan likes reading better than running." She pulled little Blair up onto her hip and baby-talked to her. "Yes, we like to hold still, don't we?" Then she turned to me, excited. "Oh, Andy, you've got to see Blair color! She grips the crayon like an adult, and can actually draw shapes."

"Wow," I said.

"Wow," Brian echoed.

Zan dug a pen out of her purse, and a little note pad. "Here, honey. Let's make a circle." She glanced at Brian and me. "Watch, you guys."

Brian sighed, but I nudged him and we politely oohed and aahed over Blair's dainty scribbles.

Last week, Zan had told me that Nolan was understanding Play-Doh. It took me three days to realize that she'd said Plato.

That night as Brian squirted toothpaste onto his toothbrush, he said, "I'm sick of those kids."

"Come on," I said. "Only twenty more years to go."

"I mean Nick's kids."

"Oh!" I laughed. "I thought you meant ours."

Brian gave me a look. "Ours are . . . *ours*. That's different."

"But I thought you liked Nolan and Blair. They're such perfect little babies—"

"That's just it," Brian groused. "I'm sick of hearing about how perfect they are."

"Well, our kids are smart, too," I said, mentally groping for a good example. I looked over at him. "Come on, they're your niece and nephew. They're family."

Brian sighed and rinsed his mouth. "Did we brag like that when we had Erica?"

"We probably bored everyone to tears," I said. "It's just something new parents do."

Brian thought for a moment. "Yes, but Erica was special."

I laughed. "She got that from her dad." Then I put my arms around Brian. "Have I told you lately how much I appreciate all the things you do for me?" We kissed and I ran a finger along Brian's jawline. "I love it how you always get gas in the cars for me."

Brian shrugged. "It's easier than leaving my class to come and pick you up."

Now I scowled and pulled away, playfully slapping Brian on the arm. "I don't find that funny," I said.

Brian smiled. "Neither do I."

"Stop humming the *I Love Lucy* theme," I snapped. I gave him my toughest glance, but couldn't fight the guilty grin on my face. Brian was right: since having triplets, my brain had taken a definite leave of absence.

The next morning after the older kids were in school, Brian indulged in a leisurely reading of the newspaper, since he had no classes that day. Suddenly he slapped the paper down on the table. "Aha!" he shouted. "Listen to this." He then read from a column by Dr. Joyce Brothers: "Super intelligent parents tend to bear children who are less intelligent than themselves, and exceptionally dull parents tend to bear youngsters brighter than themselves. This is known as 'regression toward the mean.'" He looked up, triumphant. "That's it!" he said. "From now on, our line is, 'Our kids are stupid.'"

"Brian!"

"What?" He held his hands out innocently on either side.

I shook my head. "You are beyond hope."

Just then we heard a crash and dashed into the triplets' room to find our threesome using a hand mirror to hammer pegs into a play workbench. Slivers of glass were everywhere.

"See there?" Brian said. "I rest my case."

"Oh, you and Grayson," I sputtered. "You're always resting your cases all over the place!" I turned to the children. "No one move. Hold completely still—I'll get the vacuum."

"You guys are acting like three-year-olds," Brian muttered. The boys grinned.

No sooner had we cleaned up the mirror, than Bennett found a lump of clay that he thought would look good mashed into a carved wood picture frame in the living room. Who would have thought wood and clay would not be permissible items to have within reach of a boy who's nearly four?

While I was picking clay out of the frame with a toothpick, Bennett decided to dress Gizmo in Grayson's favorite shirt. Gizmo then went outside and came in covered with mud. Austin, meanwhile, had jammed a tape into the VCR, and Brian was counting under his breath to control his temper as he tried to pry it loose. Sensing the mood accurately, Austin hightailed it for the backyard, where he flung a Frisbee onto the roof and began crying that it wouldn't come down.

While trying to reach it with a broom handle, I fell into a rose bush, and abruptly needed five Band-Aids. While I was busy applying them to my wounds (for which I was admired by all three boys), they made off with the Band-Aid box and covered the hall mirror with them. "I wonder if Edith knows what will take adhesive off a mirror," I mumbled, trying uselessly to scrape the gummy glue off with my fingernails.

"Is tonight your homemaking lesson?" Brian asked, coming around the corner.

"Oh my gosh—I completely forgot!" I said. "I've got to prepare my lesson. Quick—put a movie on for the triplets."

"Didn't we agreed not to use the television as a baby-sitter?"

I frowned. "Oh, yeah." Another family home evening goal, made during temporary insanity. "Could you take the boys someplace, then? Please? Then I'll take them this afternoon for you."

Brian sighed, glanced over the wreckage of the morning and said, "It's probably a good idea, anyway. What's your lesson on?"

"How to have quality time with your kids," I said, dashing to my desk and riffling through a stack of papers for the articles I had set aside last week. "Can you believe it—a big topic like that, and I forgot all about it?"

"Let's go to Ant Eater's house," Bennett said, using their term of endearment for "Aunt Edith."

"Not for a million bucks," Brian said. "We're going to the park." He smiled as he loaded the kids into the car.

I stood on the porch and waved as he backed out of the garage. "Take your time!" I sang.

Brian stopped and leaned out his window. "Oh, by the way, there'll be a call coming in later, from some Mother of the Year thing . . ."

I scowled. "Very funny."

In three hours the boys were back, their shoes full of sand from the park and their faces full of chocolate from the ice cream truck. Brian limped in, his hair and clothes a mess. "That curly slide is not made for adults," he mumbled as he collapsed onto the sofa.

I threw my arms around him. "Thanks," I said, "you saved the day for me. I'll take them to a matinee if you want to get some rest."

Brian slurred as he spoke. "Okay. Soundslikeagoodidea."

I laughed, cleaned up the munchkins and marched them back out to the van again. Bennett stretched out on the floor just as we were heading out the door, and I tripped over him. "What are you doing?" I asked.

"I'm a speed bump," he grinned.

Brian lurched to his feet and waved from the porch as I buckled the triplets up. "When you get back," he said, "if I'm not here, I have not gone to the Bahamas. And I will not be staying at the Royal Bahamian hotel. I've gone to the store. Yeah."

I trotted up to Brian and leaned into his face. "You go to the Bahamas without me and you're dead meat."

"Okay," he said. "You can come." Then he glanced at the bouncing silhouettes in the van. "But they stay."

I laughed and kissed him. Brian pretended to be perfectly serious. "If you smother kids, they won't grow. They need to learn independence and the value of freedom."

"What are you suggesting—leaving the gate open and shooing them out like yearling colts?"

"No, just a quick vacation for you and me. Hey, it's not like I wouldn't leave them a VISA card."

I laughed and swung my poor, tired husband around.

"I'm only half kidding," he said.

"I know."

"So what theater are you going to?" Brian asked. "In case there's an emergency and I need a young wrecking crew?"

"The mall one," I said.

Brian grimaced. "They have terrible popcorn there. Go to the cineplex."

I laughed. "You are the only man I know who goes to movies based on the theater's popcorn."

"Of course," Brian said, as if this standard were universal. "A terrible movie can be saved by good popcorn, but a good movie can be ruined by bad popcorn. That's the law." He has even been known to drive to a theater, beg his way in to buy popcorn, then run back out to his car and continue on his way.

"You don't even care what movie we're going to see?" I asked him.

"Okay, what movie?"

"It's a science fiction thriller. It's called *I Married Popcorn Man.*" I raised my hands and curled my fingers into scary claws.

Brian snarled at having walked into my trap. He pulled me close until we were nose to nose. "Oh yeah? Well, I married *Scrapbook Woman.*"

I laughed, but pretended to be insulted. "And it was a lucky thing you did," I said, "or the lives of your children would be completely undocumented." Okay, it was a weak retort, but it was the best I could do.

Brian held his hands to his cheeks in mock horror. "No!" he gasped. "Not undocumented!"

I pulled a face and got into the van. Brian pulled one back and we kept craning to pull faces at each other until I had driven away. I glanced back at the triplets, who were mimicking us perfectly. No doubt Nick's and Zan's children were above this sort of thing. Thank goodness Natalie wasn't there to comment.

As I drove to the theater, I thought about the endless volumes of scrapbooks I'd been keeping for each of the kids. I was so determined that each one feel special that I suppose I had gone a little overboard. I mean, Erica was fourteen and already she was on volume sixteen. The earlier volumes had outgrown the bookcase in the family room and were now packed in boxes and stuffed onto the shelves of a closet.

I looked back at my newest little scrapbook stars and

sighed. What will their wives think when they get married, and, as Brian predicts, they have to rent a U-Haul just to cart away the scrapbooks? "I can just picture Grayson's first date," Brian said once. "He'll bring her home and suggest looking at scrapbooks. After about an hour, he'll pick up the fifth one and say, 'And then when I was two . . .'"

"You always exaggerate," I countered, refusing to accept the fact that he was no doubt exactly right. I always thought our children's mates would coo and giggle over my meticulous efforts to save every snapshot, every tithing receipt, every crayon masterpiece. But maybe they wouldn't be like me at all.

I pictured Grayson's wife. What if she's some braless girl in a tank top with four tattoos on her arms, and when I drive up to their apartment building, she looks out the window and sneers, "Here comes Scrapbook Woman" the same way you'd say "Java Man"?

Suddenly I could see my child-rearing days pass before my eyes. There were all the traditions—the bunny cakes at Easter, the window-painting at Christmas, the stickers on the chore chart, the musical toothbrushes, the vegetable garden—all the things I was sure would become cherished memories. Suddenly I could picture my future daughters-in-law seeing me as a pain in the neck for setting a ridiculous precedent they wouldn't want to follow.

They'd see me as an aging twit who spent a lifetime making silly cakes while her sons were left unmonitored to gorge on Twinkies and Popsicles. Grayson's wife, more enlightened, would bring buckwheat dressing on Thanksgiving and soybean candy at Christmas.

Ryan's wife would be the only other woman in the universe who is more Type A than I am. She will be Type A-*plus*. She'll sigh in exasperation as I hunt through my knife drawer for a spatula. Hers will be hanging on a pegboard in their kitchen, arranged alphabetically. She will have married Ryan for his crackling wit and boundless creativity. But she will blame *me* for the fact that he wanders out onto the porch with his dinner dishes, when he knows perfectly well that they belong in the sink.

"His mother spoiled him," she'll confide to her friends.

"She followed him around reminding him what to do at every step." She'll roll her eyes when anyone mentions that Ryan was on Ritalin for Attention Deficit Disorder. Twenty years from now there would be a simpler, drug-free solution that I should somehow have known about.

Austin would marry a girl who will name their children Hip, Cool and Bomber after popular rock stars of the era. When a trace of dismay shows through my forced smile, she will accuse me of intruding and not being supportive. My baby gift of a doll will be seen as perpetuating sexist stereotypes. "It's so *last century*," she'll whisper to friends.

As Bennett's wife brings each new bundle home, she'll laugh at my outdated parenting information. After all, in two more decades, the experts will have changed everything again. Talcum powder will not be cancer-causing after all; it will increase I.Q. Breast-feeding will be out of style, in favor of synthetic milks (invented by Edith) that guarantee Olympic track stars.

And what will most annoy Cameron's wife is having to watch hours and hours of videotape starring Cameron the Childhood Ham. (Arguments over whose baby videos to watch will emerge as the leading cause of divorce twenty years from now.) I, of course, will be the culprit for holding the camera.

And then, in the cruelest blow of all, there will be a television talk show whose theme of the day is, "Toxic Mothers-in-Law: Could Yours Be One?" All five of my daughters-in-law will be on it, and stage hands with dollies will haul in sixty scrapbooks as evidence.

Brian and I will be watching from our rockers in the rest home and Brian will mumble, "I was afraid of this."

"Mommy! Mommy!" The triplets broke into my trance, and I realized we were already at the theater. (I vaguely realized that they had been arguing over whether the proper response to Mommy coming down the hallway was "yikes" or "yipes.")

"Oh—right," I mumbled as I led them to the ticket window. "Six, please. I mean three. I mean four," I said.

"Which is it?" the fellow behind the glass asked.

I sighed. "Three kids and one very tired adult."

CHAPTER 13

THE GOSPEL
ACCORDING TO EDITH

Edith woke us up one morning, calling from Tokyo, to ask Brian if she could speak in a sacrament meeting to share her "theory of activity." Brian rubbed his eyes. "You're asking if you can give a talk?" he croaked, trying to wake up.

"That's right," I could hear Edith's loud voice bleeding through the receiver.

Brian shrugged. "Sure. I'll ask the bishop . . . No, I am not passing the buck, Edith . . . Yes, I know you have a lot to say . . . Okay, Edith . . . okay." He hung up and collapsed back onto his pillow. "How," he began softly, building his volume until he was screaming, "can someone so crazy WIN THE NOBEL PRIZE?"

I patted his chest. "I'm sure she doesn't know what time it is here."

"You check these things out," Brian said, struggling to regain his composure. "I'll bet this is the first time in history that someone has volunteered to give a talk in our ward. Maybe in any ward in the Church. And they have to call me at five in the morning. From Japan."

"She's really popular over there with the electronics people. And her song is number one there, I think."

"Good. Then let her wake *them* up." Brian rolled over and punched his pillow. "What's she going to talk about—how to get to heaven using Frequent Flyer mileage?"

"Maybe you can assign her a topic."

"Ha. As if anyone has ever reined Edith Horvitz in. She'll digress within thirty seconds."

I smiled. I liked Edith more all the time. "Maybe she could talk on visiting teaching," I said. "I know Edith really likes her visiting teacher."

Brian sighed and drifted back to sleep.

A month later Edith was sitting on the stand, and jumped right up when it was time for her to speak. "I'm glad I was invited to speak today," Edith began. Brian glanced at me from the corner of his eyes.

"I've been asked to talk about visiting teaching," Edith went on. "This and home teaching are the most important jobs in the Church," she said. "When we try to help other people, that's when we practice what we learn at church."

I smiled; Edith was doing great. She talked about being Christ's hands and feet in doing good for others. She praised her own visiting teacher, who was "almost like a lab assistant," running errands to pick up Edith's various chemicals from the pharmacy. "Well, except when she refused to hold those copper wires that time," Edith said. "It wouldn't have been that many volts, either. But anyway, I really appreciate her."

Erica stared at me in embarrassment, as if I had written Edith's remarks for her.

Edith continued. "You know what amazes me?" she said. "People who think they can only visit someone just like themselves. Imagine if I were that way," Edith said. "I'd have nobody to visit!" Some snickers rolled forward; Edith was well aware that she was one-of-a-kind.

"How the heck can you grow and learn if you only visit easy people, active people, people your same age, people who are just like you? No offense, but that sounds pretty boring to me."

I glanced at Brian. His nostrils were flaring as Edith strayed from her notes and began to wing it.

"When you're asked to visit somebody," she said, "it's because that's who the Lord wants you to see. Imagine a missionary refusing to go where he gets sent because he doesn't have anything in common with folks there! Imagine him calling up the prophet and asking for a different assignment. What a crybaby."

Yikes—I could see several women who had asked for such reassignments stiffening as they listened. But Edith wasn't through. "I've been assigned all kinds of sisters," Edith said, "and I love it. Variety's good for you. Take my diet."

Uh-oh. Big derailment. Edith took a minute to tell about her birdseed, then found her way back to the assigned topic. "Isn't it crazy when women ask for a certain kind of sister to visit? What do they think this is—computer dating?" Edith snorted. "You're there to serve. Period. Imagine some people in a capsized boat, and in comes a Coast Guard helicopter to rescue them. Only first, the pilot has to make sure he has enough in common with them." She then pretended to be shouting through a megaphone down to the shivering victims. "So what kind of music do you guys like? You like pizza? How about sports—you guys sports fans?"

By now everyone was cracking up, and Edith grinned. "And we're not gonna convince anybody we really care about them if we wait until the end of the month to call them. Think about your own home teacher or visiting teacher. If they wait until the end of the month, do you feel important to them? Or like a number?"

Now all was silent.

"Just as I thought," Edith said. "You know the one trait most needed in this church? I mean, Church members have lots of great traits already. They're loving, happy, generous, sincere—I could go on and on. But you know what we need more of? Folks you can count on. People who are defensible."

"You mean dependable?" Brian whispered behind her.

"That's right," Edith said. "Dependable. That's the keyhole of religion. If you say you're gonna do it, then do it. But don't say you will and then let people down. That drives me crazy."

So that's what did it.

"Getting back to service," Edith said, "I like to help the grouches. You know why? Because I figure they might be mentally ill, and I feel sorry for them. I might be the only person all day who smiles at them." Everyone was laughing again, but Edith was serious. "And maybe I can undo some of the bad examples they're setting for the Church. Grouches are reverse missionaries, y'know. It's true. You get one grouchy Mormon out there in public, and you'll have ten people walk away from him vowing never to join *that* church!

"You've heard of Einstein's theory of relativity? Well, I'm gonna give you Edith's theory of activity. This is gonna keep you guys from slipping into apostrophe."

Did she mean apostasy?

"Any of you folks who are thinking of becoming inactive," Edith continued, "you might want to reconsider, and here's why. You're needed to counteract all the grouches! Just like acids and bases, folks. We've got all these sour, dour crybabies out there, and we need every one of us to be happy and cheerful, just to cancel out their poor examples."

I liked Edith's talk so much I almost applauded. She only digressed one more time, and I thoroughly agreed with her point.

"I'd like to know," she said, "how it is that a Boy Scout can build a birdhouse, wire a doorbell, and survive in the wilderness, but he can't even sew on his own badges! That ought to be the first requirement for becoming a Cub Scout—thread a needle. How come the moms get roped into sewing dozens of these little doodahs onto all those shirts? If *I* was running things, the deal would be, 'If you can't sew it on, you can't have it.'" Every mom in the chapel was beaming.

Edith then concluded and sat down beside Brian, patting his knee, which he jerked away. As he stared at me, I knew he was blaming me for picking a topic on which Edith had such strong views. But then, Edith had strong views on every topic.

Rain was predicted that Sunday, and though we'd made it to church before the cloudburst, I had brought three umbrellas for the kids to share and had placed them under our bench. Unfortunately, I had been so engrossed in Edith's talk that I hadn't seen the triplets get their hands on them. Now, suddenly, as if they were secretly Rockettes, the triplets opened them right there in the chapel. Fwap! Fwap! Fwap! Red! Yellow! Blue! Erica, Grayson and I mobilized like trained militia, trying to wrestle the umbrellas closed. The spokes of

Grayson's umbrella stuck Sister Mahoney's elderly blue curls and she let out a yelp.

"I'm so sorry," I whispered. Then Erica's spokes got caught in the knit dress of the woman behind us, lifting her skirt up. Naturally, she screamed and fought to re-cover her legs.

I looked up at Brian. He looked dead, like a cardboard cutout of a first counselor that had been rolled in as a prop.

Finally, sweating rivers, we got the umbrellas closed and put away. I stole a peek at Brian, who I knew would not find any of this amusing. Now he was holding an imaginary remote control and pointing it at the triplets. "Click! Click! Click!" he mouthed.

Everyone in the chapel laughed, and I slid down in my seat.

Erica was the picture of pain, no doubt blaming me for bringing the umbrellas in the first place. "This is like pack meeting all over again," she whispered. Last month Ryan had received his Arrow of Light award, and the triplets had sneaked onto the stage ahead of time, somehow found a bottle of Clorox that someone had used in a demonstration of emergency preparedness (only they forgot to bring an empty one), and dragged it behind the target just before the ceremony. When the scoutmaster shot the arrow, it went right through the bull's-eye and into the bleach bottle. Needless to say, bleach ran everywhere and soaked into the hem of the stage's red velvet curtain. For a week the cultural hall reeked of bleach and the curtain looked as if someone had tried to tie-dye the bottom pink. On the other hand, the rags from the custodian's closet were never so clean.

During the sacrament meeting's closing song, I tried to soften Brian's anguish by winking at him and smiling seductively. He chewed his cheek, then finally smiled back at me. As his eyes returned to the hymn book, I widened my focus and realized that Bishop Johansson was staring at me, horrified. Seated right beside Brian, he must have thought I was winking and kissing at him! I gulped.

Right after the meeting I dashed up to Brian. "You have to tell the bishop I was not making eyes at him," I whispered, feeling tears well up in my eyes.

"Oh, not this again," Brian said, stuffing his hands into his pockets. "Listen, I'm the one who ought to be embarrassed—my sons opening umbrellas during—"

"I am *much* more embarrassed than you are," I argued, pulling Brian's arm and trying to aim him at the bishop.

Brian took a deep breath. "Andy, how come you're always at the root of all embarrassment?"

Erica happened to walk by at that moment and stopped. "Yeah," she said. "How come?"

I sighed and begged Brian again. "Pleeease?"

"Oh, all right." Brian turned to deliver my message as I darted out with Erica. "Please don't walk me to class, Mom," she said, scooting ahead of me and almost jogging away.

"Oh. Right," I said, and hung back. Sometimes I felt I just couldn't do anything that wasn't embarrassing Erica. Over the past six months she had issued specific instructions to me to avoid embarrassing her. I must never wave from the car to anyone she knows. In fact, I should refrain from waving to anyone, anytime. I should not buy any clothing, makeup or personal items for her if anyone can possibly see me. I should wear makeup every day, especially if I'm planning to look out of any window where someone might catch a glimpse of me. I should never, ever dance. I should not sing to the radio, or even sing very loudly at church. And I should not try to dress cool, because I am most decidedly not.

Brian was not exempt from her eye-rolling reactions. She recently made the announcement that she didn't like his job. Being a history professor was "the worst," she informed us.

"Why can't you have a cool job like Kayla's dad?" Kayla's father was a stuntman for the movies.

"Gee, I don't know," Brian said, "There's just something about going over a cliff in a car that explodes in midair . . ."

Erica rolled her eyes again. "See? Now that's cool." When I pointed out the fact that Kayla's father was in the hospital for his third surgery this year, and that there wasn't a joint in his body that wasn't filled with enough pins to set off a metal detector, Erica just looked at me as if I had suggested she wear swimming goggles as a fashion item. "You just don't understand how cool that is," she said.

That night as I was smoothing moisturizer on my face, Brian said, "I spoke to the bishop for you."

"Oh, thank you so much, honey. What did he say?"

"He says he's worried about you. You have this compulsion to throw yourself at him."

I whirled around. "He did not!"

Brian laughed. "Why do you put so much junk on your face?"

I patted a second cream around my eyes. "To keep from getting wrinkled."

Brian sighed. "None of that stuff works, you know. Wrinkles are genetic."

"This one does," I said. "Says so right here on the label. So what did the bishop really say?"

"He hadn't even noticed you." Brian took a drink of water. "Maybe his look was because he was still aghast over the umbrella show. The Andy Taylor Dancers."

As we got into bed, I snuggled up to Brian, relieved that Bishop Johansson hadn't seen me.

"Do you realize," Brian said, gently stroking my lubricated cheek, "that if we had a house fire, your face would fry?"

I slapped his arm and pulled back, sputtering as I tried to think of a comeback. "How can you be such a . . . a stupe?" I asked.

Brian laughed, then looked at me and said, "Oh, yeah? What do you mean by *that?*"

Now I laughed and fell on top of him, tickling his sides. I rubbed my cheeks on his as he tried to pull away. "Yuuuck!" he snarled.

"You're so farsighted," I said, "you've never actually seen me. Do you know that?"

"So, if you're wrinkled enough to need all that junk, be glad." He had a point there.

Just then we heard a creaking in the hall. "What are the kids doing?" I whispered.

Brian sighed. "Gee, I don't know. Ever since I was shot by that kryptonite bullet, I can't see through the walls."

Gizmo came walking into the room, his collar jingling softly. "I guess it was just the dog," I said.

"How come you always get wired and want to talk when it's time to go to sleep?" Brian asked. "You should sue the Church for exclusive rights to use the word *fireside*. That's what you conduct every night. Just like FDR."

"I'm just too exhausted to sleep."

Brian rolled over. "Pretend you're at a funeral and I'm the speaker."

"Very funny," I said. "You'd better watch out." I lifted a toy of Ryan's out from under my side of the bed. It was a contraption made of cardboard tubes and duct tape. Edith would be proud. "Or I'll blast you."

"What is that?" Brian asked.

"Ryan says it's an all-purpose bazooka."

"Let's see it," Brian said, taking it and putting it on his nightstand. "I'll use it next time Edith calls and wakes us up."

I snuggled up to Brian and slowly drifted off. Popcorn Man and Scrapbook Woman, asleep at last.

CHAPTER 14

VIDEO MOM

The next morning the phone rang and woke us up, this time at five-thirty.

"If that's Edith again . . ." Brian said. But it was Natalie calling for me.

"Guess what?" she sang. "I'm getting married!"

Her new boyfriend, Gorman, had proposed to her the previous night, but since it was so late she waited until morning to call. "I knew you'd be up with the kids," she said, "and I haven't slept all night. I'm so excited!"

"Well, that's . . . wonderful!" I said. Gorman was even LDS, a rarity in Natalie's dating world. I'd never met him, but Natalie said he was a terrific guy.

"Haven't they only known each other a month?" Brian asked.

"What can I say?" I yawned. "She's in love."

"She didn't ask us to help, I hope," Brian said, remembering Nick's wedding.

"You're such a romantic."

Brian shrugged. "Hey, wait a second. Doesn't Gorman have kids?"

"Just one son. I think he's almost grown. Lives mostly with his mother," I said, trying to go back to sleep.

"Who—Gorman?"

"No," I groaned, wishing Brian would stop asking questions. "The son lives with Gorman's ex-wife."

"I thought Natalie didn't want to get married." Brian was wide awake now, which meant I would soon follow suit.

"Maybe she just never met the right person before."

"But how can she know if he's the right person if they've only known each other a month?"

I sat up. "What is this, the verbal equivalent to 'Found a Peanut'? We're right back where we started."

"Oh." Brian rolled over. "I just think it's kind of sudden." THEN HE FELL BACK ASLEEP!

I knew it was useless for me to try to get back to sleep again; my mind was already gearing up for the task of listening to my mother's worries over this latest ripple in her placid pond. And sure enough, she called just as Brian had taken the older kids to school.

"We know nothing about this Gorman person," Mother said, as if he were applying for Nick's old job as an intelligence agent.

"Natalie says he's a great guy," I said, knowing my comments were simply punctuation so that Mom could continue.

"And he's a podiatrist. What kind of man becomes a podiatrist, anyway?"

"A guy who likes feet, I suppose."

"Exactly. And what kind of person likes feet?"

I sighed, glanced at the time and tried to figure a way to end the conversation.

"See?" Mom went on. "He's probably a nut of some kind."

"Mom, just because the man is a foot doctor—"

"Well, he's not going to get his hands on my feet, I'll tell you that right now. I don't trust him."

"Mom, you haven't even met him. And anyway, your feet are probably the last thing on his mind."

"What's wrong with my feet?"

"Nothing! Oh—the triplets are trying to pour their own milk. I'll talk to you later. Bye!"

The phone rang again immediately, and I let the answering machine pick it up while I mopped milk and cereal off the floor. It was Mom again. "I forgot to tell you something," she said. "The Halperts might be moving. Keep your fingers crossed."

The Halperts were Mom's next-door neighbors, and she'd

been nursing a lively feud with them for six years now. When I realized it had become an obsession, I decided to have a chat with Mom, and urge her to forgive the list of offenses that seemed to grow every time we spoke. "If you can't forgive them and get past all this," I said, "your own spiritual growth will suffer. Just look how they bring your temper out."

She glared over her glasses at me. "The Lord will understand," she had huffed. "Once I'm away from those horrible people, there won't be anyone to bring my temper out! They'll go to the bottom kingdom and I'll be in the celestial kingdom, away from such individuals."

Wow! She had somehow managed to judge this family's fate, twist the gospel into a granny knot, and speak for the Lord himself, all in one breath.

And now she was calling with the news that her test was moving away. I wished the Halperts would stay until Mom could learn forgiveness. It's strange how some people can create a logic all their own to justify their choices.

I thought of the women I'd counseled and worked with in Relief Society. So many of them needed a change of heart—and a *softening* of heart, too. Some were paralyzed by self-pity and unmet expectations. They somehow had the warped idea that life was to be one big party, and they were to be the guests of honor. They felt entitled to special treatment. Then, ironically, there were women whose confidence was so low that you couldn't convince them of their own worth as children of God. These sisters felt they didn't deserve to be happy. Both groups moped through life, one feeling they deserved more and another feeling they deserved less. Both were wasting a great deal of human potential.

Then there were members like my mother, who were too confident of their free ride into exaltation. They thought they could coast in on their baptismal certificates without ever working to conquer personal weaknesses or serving unconditionally. Mother considers herself perfectly active, yet she refuses to teach Primary. "I've served," she chirps.

And there was a counterpart group to this one: sisters who were truly doing their best with good hearts and willing hands, yet who heaped guilt upon themselves and refused to rejoice in the atoning sacrifice of the Savior—women who were convinced they'd never "make it." It amazed me how the gospel—so simple and perfect—could get misconstrued in such opposite directions. As Edith would say, waving her triple combination from the podium (as she did at a recent fast and testimony meeting), "If you want to know how to live your life, you gotta read the instructions!"

Natalie, on the other hand, chose to read travel brochures. She spent no time whatsoever planning her wedding, but focused instead upon the honeymoon. As soon as she and Gorman had confirmed their reservations to Fiji and New Zealand, they eloped and headed to the airport. Brian and I learned of the marriage from a 3-D postcard featuring a tattooed Fiji warrior with his tongue sticking out. "Surprise," it read, "we got married!"

Brian studied the postcard. "I guess this guy is showing us the appropriate reaction we are to have."

I sighed. It was definitely the most unusual wedding announcement we had ever received.

"Cool," Ryan said, breezing by. "Can I have the stamp?"

My mother, luckily, received her "surprise" on a postcard showing a beach. If she'd gotten one like ours, I think it might have done her in. Still, she was pretty upset. "This is no way to announce a marriage," she snapped, tossing the card on my kitchen counter as I cleaned up after a triplet finger-painting extravaganza. "And," mother said, pausing for dramatic effect, "there are *foot*prints on that beach." She smirked. "Who else but a podiatrist would pick such a card to announce a marriage?"

Mom had come over to watch the triplets while I went on a Saturday date with Grayson. Brian and I had been making it a top priority to spend one-on-one time with each of the kids, and once a month we each went on a special date with them. Usually the kids chose the activity, and today Grayson and I headed for a video arcade. (This has to beat hog heads, I thought to myself, recalling Ryan's macabre choice last week to visit a butcher shop.)

As we walked in, I tried not to cringe visibly. The room

was filled with sloppily dressed, shaggy-looking adolescents who appeared to be going nowhere as quickly as possible. I felt like a true fuddy-duddy sizing them up the way I did; but as I looked at their gaping mouths and glazed expressions, I couldn't help thinking that their combined GPAs couldn't get you into Clown College. And this was my son's idea of an ideal afternoon.

"Well," I said, trying to sound cheery, "which machine do we play first?"

Grayson squinted at me. "There's not an order to it, Mom."

Duh—like these people would be here if there were? I smiled. "I meant, which one do you want to play first?"

Grayson led me to a row of television monitors encased in garishly painted plastic. "This is an easy one. Try it," he said.

Hey, I thought to myself, if I wanted to feel like a dummy, I could go over to Edith Horvitz's and thumb through her notebooks. But I smiled at Grayson; at least he was not too embarrassed to be here with his mom. It was actually a great compliment; I felt as if Grayson were letting me into a special club.

"This is Sunset Riders," Grayson said. "You just shoot everything."

"Those are the instructions?"

Grayson nodded and we began to play. Within a few seconds Grayson had a zillion points, my cowboy was gored by a charging bull (upon which Grayson's cowboy deftly leaped), and the game ended.

"Let's try Rampage," Grayson said. "You just punch everything."

"That's it?"

"That's it." Grayson seemed content with this lack of complexity. He inserted the game tokens and began helping a gorilla destroy a skyscraper. Within seconds Grayson had pulverized several urban structures and helicopters, while my gorilla shrank to the size of a thumbnail and sidled away in naked humiliation.

"Let's do some more challenging games," I said, "and I'll just watch you."

"You don't want to play? They have pinball machines in the corner."

No, I do not want to hide in the remedial section. "I'd like to see you play some of the harder ones," I said. Grayson shrugged and instantly headed for the machines with extra bells and whistles. I checked my watch and sighed. I glanced back at the front door, where a neon sign said "Video Heaven." Boy, is that ever an oxymoron, I thought.

Between games I said to Grayson, "Do you think they'll have video games in heaven?"

"That *is* heaven," he said. "I bet they'll have the best ones ever."

How can that be? I wondered. For Grayson, heaven won't be heaven without video games; and for me, heaven won't be heaven *with* them. Surely there's a way to please everyone. There must be a separate section where it snows for people who love the cold, and where it's dry and hot for desert lovers. Brian and I will have a house that's specially designed with a double thermostat; he'll think it's wonderfully cool while I think it's toasty and warm. Perhaps there will be video games for Grayson, too; but they'll be invisible to me.

As I drifted back from my existential musings, I noticed three other boys waiting for a turn at Grayson's machine. Soon two more gathered around, watching as Grayson's hands flew through the commands. Then two big guys, who looked like they could play for the Lakers, stopped and watched. Suddenly I realized that these guys weren't waiting for a turn; they were watching Grayson beat the machine!

"He's good," one kid whispered.

"I've never seen anyone beat this before," said another boy who looked as if he possibly lived here.

I stood back to make room as a total of twelve kids gathered around. As I wandered to the side, I caught a glimpse of Grayson's face as he played. He was the picture of intense concentration. Suddenly the machine made a futuristic laser sound and a colorful blast filled the screen. A robotic voice announced that Grayson had defeated all the armies of the universe.

The boys were shouting, "All right!" and "Way to go," slapping him with high fives. Completely swept up in the excitement, I screamed, "Yea!! You did it, honey!" Various stunned teenagers turned to stare at me as I exulted, "That's my son!" to one, and "I'm his mom," to another. I was as proud as if he had just won an Olympic decathlon. "Oh, you were so terrific, honey," I continued, squeezing Grayson's shoulders and almost kissing him on the cheek.

"Wow," I babbled as Grayson slinked away from the other kids, "I had no idea video games were so exciting! My goodness, it's like you could be the national champion or something."

"Mom—"

"I'll bet you could enter a tournament or—"

"MOM!" Grayson said, finally interrupting my tirade. "I think I get your point. I think every guy *here* gets your point."

I bit my lip, realizing I had just become a stage mother. "I'm so sorry, Grayson. I was just so proud of you—"

Grayson glanced at the other kids from the corner of his eyes, saw that the coast was clear and sighed. "It's okay. But maybe, if you could, like, not do that next time . . ."

I promised, and we redeemed his prize tickets for a baseball cap, a squirt gun and a rubber spider. Then I took Grayson to an ice cream parlor to celebrate his victory with a double fudge sundae.

"It's a special occasion," I told the waitress, a girl with trolls sewn on her tennis shoes who looked as though she couldn't care less. I waited for her to stop smacking her gum and ask what the occasion was, but since she didn't, I said, "This is my son, Grayson, and he just beat—what was the name of that game, honey?"

Grayson sat across the table from me, sliding slowly down in his seat and turning a pale shade of purple. "Mom, please . . ." he whispered.

I smiled. "Sorry." Once in the car, I apologized again. Grayson remained hunched down in his jacket and muttered the obligatory "I forgive you."

"Still buddies?"

"Yeah."

"I guess I just didn't realize how exciting it would be to

watch one of my children do something I could never do," I said.

"Mom," Grayson said wearily, counting on his fingers, "you said the same thing with T-ball, soccer, karate, computers, chess and piano."

I glanced sideways at him. "So you're saying I ought to be used to being shown up by now, and not have to tell everyone about it."

Grayson smiled at me. "Something like that."

I smiled as we drove along, basking in the joy of my son's excellence. "Nah," I said. "I can't imagine keeping a secret that good."

CHAPTER 15

DIAL-A-DISASTER

The next week my ineptitude was reinforced yet again, this time by Ryan's math homework. I was still his scribe, writing down whatever he told me as he calculated the answers.

"Cross out the nine there and borrow one for the two, to make it twelve," I said.

"That's not the new way, Mom."

"Oh, yes it is," I said. "I was taught New Math in school."

Ryan snickered. "Yeah, and Harry Truman was the new president once."

Here we go again, I thought. Mary Migraine helps her son with his math, as he helps her over the brink. That night in bed—the only chance for conversation that Brian and I ever seem to have—I told him that Ryan had compared me to Harry Truman.

Brian shrugged. "I've compared you to FDR."

"How many women are compared to dead presidents?" I sputtered. "Unattractive dead presidents, I might add."

"What's your point?"

"Would you stop asking me what my point is?" I snapped.

Brian sighed. "So how do you think Ryan's doing on the new dosage?" Yesterday the doctor had increased his Ritalin.

"Same," I said. "His teacher said he pulled a dead lizard out of his desk today."

Brian shook his head. "How did *that* get in there?"

I just looked at him. "Well, it seems the poor thing left a suicide note explaining everything."

Brian sighed and bunched up his pillow under his head.

"Ryan asked Matt Nemick to sleep over Friday," I said. "What time shall I tell his parents to pick him up?

"Dawn."

"C'mon, Brian. People like to have a restful Saturday morning."

"I *know*."

I started giggling.

"Don't start this," Brian said. "Once you start giggling you don't stop for fifteen minutes."

"Yes I do," I said, stuffing part of the blanket into my mouth to stifle the sound.

"Why is there a sleep over of some kind every weekend? And why do they always come here?" Brian asked.

I tried to wind back down again. "Oh, I've encouraged that," I said. "I'd much rather have their friends here in our home, where I know what they're doing and watching on television, than let our kids go to someone else's house."

Brian just stared at me. "You mean this is by *design?* Our house has become a youth hostel on *purpose?*" Brian rolled onto his back as if shot by a rifle.

Now I began giggling again. "The only thing hostile about this is you," I said. "Are you telling me that you'd rather have the kids go to someone else's house?"

"Of course!"

"Oh."

Brian pounced on me, tickling me until I begged for mercy.

Finally we both slumped onto our pillows. "Let's set some policies," Brian said. "We will permit our children to visit their friends' homes. Agreed?"

"Okay."

"In fact," Brian went on, "we will encourage it at every opportunity."

"Brian . . ."

"And we will never ground them."

"Why not?"

"Are you kidding?" Brian said. "Why should *we* suffer?"

I rolled my eyes. "You are ridiculous."

"Well, that's what happens when you ride around in a car

all day with triplets who scream 'BUG!' every five seconds."

I laughed. The younger boys, now almost four, were obsessed with spotting Volkswagens and would shout "BUG!" whenever they saw one. With three kids all competing and quarreling over who saw one first, it could get pretty chaotic.

"I'd like to get my hands on the culprit who taught them that stupid game," Brian muttered.

I swallowed silently in the darkness.

"I heard that," Brian said. "It was you, wasn't it?"

"Well, it *does* teach counting," I said.

Brian sprang up to tickle me again. "To the finish," he snarled in my ear.

"No," I shrieked, laughing before he could even touch me. "Please! I'm too tired."

Brian fell back onto his side of the bed. "Me, too," he said. "And to think I've been blaming the kids for all my problems."

"No, you already had a lot of them when I met you," I agreed.

Brian kissed my neck. "So how did the school project go?"

I cringed. I had forgotten all about that morning's fiasco. I had volunteered to teach a Valentine craft to Ryan's class, and decided to show them something I had just learned at homemaking meeting. It was a woven heart valentine made from red and white construction paper, and when you're through it opens like a pocket. I thought it would be just adorable filled with little heart candies.

Brian had watched me preparing the materials earlier, and had said, "A lot of adults couldn't weave that thing. Why not do something simpler?"

I smiled confidently and gestured toward another stack of red and white sheets of paper. "It just so happens that I *do* have a simpler option," I said. "If they think the pocket is too hard, they can just make simple, woven, heart-shaped place mats."

Brian shook his head. "Ten of those kids are going to need shock therapy after today."

"Oh, they will not," I countered. Brian is such an exaggerator.

"And the rest will run away from home and join the circus," he predicted. "Nobody's going to be able to make that thing.

"They will when *I* teach them," I said. "I have a way with kids."

Two hours later I was standing before Ryan's class, which had exploded into complete chaos, listening to the wailing and gnashing of his frustrated classmates—every one of whom had picked the pocket over the place mat. The children were all screaming at the tops of their lungs, and all at me:

How do you get the white piece under the red one?

I can't, I can't! This is too hard!!

Mine tore!

Will you do mine?

I don't get it!

One boy even burst into tears and slumped over his desk, wailing.

"Maybe some of them should have picked the place mat," I whispered to another room mom who was there to help (but who stood aside and let me flounder alone).

"Let me tell you something about kids," she said testily, as if I'd never met one before. "They will always pick the more complicated thing."

I glanced at Ryan, who was shrinking down into his seat.

Finally I ended up weaving everybody's pocket for them, then slinking out of the room to the sound of subsiding sniffles. So much for holiday merriment.

I turned to answer Brian. "It was . . . it was . . ."

"I knew it," Brian said. "How many mothers called this afternoon who want us to pay for their kids' psychotherapy?"

"It was so awful," I winced, my voice almost squeaking as I recalled the pain of it all. "One kid even cried, and another one tore hers up and threw it."

Now Brian was laughing. "You wouldn't listen."

"But I thought it would be so fun," I whimpered. "What a disaster."

"Sorry I missed it."

"Sorry I didn't."

"Well, I guess you're out of the running for Best Room Mother," he said.

I sighed. "And to think I had it all sewn up until today."

CHAPTER 16

INTO THE FIRE

Natalie had returned from her honeymoon and had asked to come over Monday night to introduce Gorman. Brian was already privately calling him "Mr. Natalie."

Erica was teaching our family home evening lesson that night, and chose the topic of physical fitness. "Wear sweats," she had instructed us, since she was the only family member with leotards. She decided to put the rest of us through some of the torture she had willingly endured in ballet class, and by the end of her lesson I was ready for traction. Even my muscles' distant cousins in Des Moines were sore. Brian was disgustingly invigorated, not even winded. Grayson and Ryan had jumped at the challenge to show off their strength, and were keeping right up with Erica's regimen. The triplets, naturally, seized this opportunity as a free-for-all Wrestle Mania show, and were tumbling all over the family room.

It wasn't long before my unshared prophecy at the beginning of the lesson came true, and the triplets knocked over and broke a lamp. Brian picked up the pieces as I wiped the noses of the unhurt but loudly wailing triplets, using some tissues that had been in my purse so long that they had all but turned to powder. "It was an accident," I said to calm them down. "But we need to be careful, don't we?"

The kitchen phone rang in the middle of this commotion. Erica reached for it and knocked over Ryan's bottle of Ritalin, which must not have been capped properly, and somehow spilled the pills all over the floor. As I dashed for the pills, Gizmo beat me to it and gulped one down before I could catch him.

"This proves it!" Brian growled. "That dog will eat anything that hits the floor! How much are those things worth—about five bucks apiece?"

"Dad!" Erica shrieked, hanging up the phone. "How could you worry about money at a time like this? One of those could kill Gizmo!"

Horrified, the triplets began crying all the louder.

"Quick," Grayson yelled, grabbing our poor dog by the throat, "get it out!" He looked around, waiting for one of us to reach into the jaws of death and pull out the Ritalin tablet. "Well?" he snapped, irritated that none of us would help him.

"Stop it," Erica snapped, pulling Grayson away from Gizmo. "You're choking him!"

"Let's make him throw up," Ryan said. "I'll get the Ipecac."

"You will do no such thing," I shouted. Inducing a dog—who throws up at least ten times his quota already—to throw up yet again? Not on your life.

"Let's call Brother Patterson," Brian said. "He's a vet; he'll know if this is an emergency or not."

Just then the doorbell rang. Ryan opened the door, and Natalie and her new husband walked in to join our happy little family gathering. The triplets were bawling at the tops of their lungs. Erica—in tights and ballet slippers—was pacing hysterically and shrieking, "Are you just going to let him *die?*" Grayson was clutching the collar of a drooling dog who was straining against him to sniff our visitors. Brian was holding a broken lamp. And I was standing in the midst of it all with my hands full of narcotics.

"Gorman, we've been looking forward to meeting you," I said.

He looked like cement.

Natalie was clearly appalled, and looked from one to the other of us with horror.

"The boys just had a little accident," Brian explained, chuckling to play it down as he dumped the lamp into a waste basket with a loud crash.

"We were just going to call a veterinarian," I said. "Our dog swallowed a Ritalin tablet."

"Well, which is it?" Natalie asked, looking from me to Brian and waiting for us to pick one of our flimsy excuses.

"Both," the kids said.

Gorman hesitantly smiled. "How many milligrams?"

Oh, that's right, I thought, Gorman's a doctor! "Ten," I told him.

"He'll be all right," Gorman said, patting Gizmo's head and letting Giz' lick his hand. "He might be a little lethargic, then he'll snap out of it."

Erica sighed dramatically and slapped her hand over her heart. "Thank goodness!"

Gorman patted Gizmo again and said, "Won'tcha, fella?" Well, a man can hardly make a better first impression, I thought. A dog-lover and a hero all in one. Gorman stood up and took note of my sweatshirt. "Oh—did you go to the Sorbonne?" he asked.

"No," I sighed. "It's just a souvenir that I—"

Just then, in walked a tan, teenaged surfer with nearly white hair that swung into his eyes and down to his shoulders. He was wearing a tank top, surfer shorts and thongs, as though he'd just been strolling on a beach in Maui when aliens somehow transported him to our entryway.

"This is Chad," Natalie said. "Gorman's son. He's sixteen."

Chad grunted. His tank top had a picture of a bloody skull on it, and he was wearing a shark's tooth earring.

Erica somehow floated up to the entryway and flashed her newly-straightened smile at Chad. "Hi," she said. "I'm Erica."

Now Chad grinned, his head bobbing as if he were wearing imaginary headphones and listening to a steady beat. "Yo," he said, taking note of Erica's lithe dimensions in her leotards.

I glanced at Brian, whose pupils were turning into little red knots at this scene.

"Dessert, anyone?" I babbled, pulling Erica into the kitchen to help me cut the cake I had made for refreshments. I had taken a cake decorating class at homemaking night a few months ago, and my unpracticed hand had scrawled "Congratulations Natalie and Gorman" in some of the wobbliest lettering ever to grace a sponge cake. Even the frosting rosettes had melted into polka dots the size of nickels.

"How cute," Natalie said. "You let the kids decorate it."

I rummaged for forks as the kids all looked quizzically at one another, wondering which of them had been given this privilege.

Gizmo whimpered and slumped down under a chair. Ryan tried to pull the chair out, but Gizmo gave him a tired glance and flopped his head down on his paws.

"I think we're on to something with that dog," Brian whispered to me.

"Shh . . . it's made him depressed or something," I said.

"And that lifts *my* mood," Brian whispered back. He'd been waiting years for Gizmo to outgrow the bouncy, chewing puppy phase.

All through dessert Natalie and Gorman raved about the sparkling water and lush vistas of Fiji and New Zealand, while Brian glowered at Chad and craned his head around to watch the boy's every move.

Erica alternately smiled and blushed when their eyes met.

Just as I was sure Brian was going to burst a blood vessel, Natalie announced that they all had to be going since Chad was due at his mother's house.

Brian leaped to his feet and swung the front door open in a move I was sure Erica's ballet instructor would find remarkable. "Well, congratulations again," he said to Gorman. "You two make a great couple."

"Yes, we're so glad we finally met you," I said. Then to Natalie, "You've got a great guy." She hugged his arm and smiled.

As soon as the door closed, I motioned to Brian to save his comments, then pulled Erica into the kitchen to help me with the dishes. Gizmo groaned and sighed, as if relieved that the company had finally left. I patted his head and tried to soothe him.

"How come *I* have to clean up?" Erica whined.

Because your father needs to calm down before you hear anything he has to say, I thought to myself. The worst thing in the world right now would be for Brian to start blasting and bombasting about Chad. It would make that kid more appealing than ever.

We started rinsing dishes, and I waited for Erica to say, "Mom, thank you so much for teaching me correct principles! I'd never let some misguided soul like that lead me astray." It was quite a wait, as you might guess. I tried to dampen her interest in Chad by classifying him as a relative. "So," I said, "you have a new cousin."

Erica laughed. "Mom, he's not a cousin!"

I started rinsing dishes. "Of course he is. His father is married to Aunt Natalie."

"Well, through marriage, maybe. But that doesn't really count."

"Count how?"

"Well, like, *count*," Erica said. Again, the unspoken "duh."

In other words, this boy was available to have a crush on. I cringed. Erica smiled the entire time we were loading dishes into the dishwasher, and I knew it wasn't from the intrinsic joy of a job well done.

"Chad has his driver's license!" she said. So far, I thought.

Her eyes were twinkling the way yours or mine would if someone had said, "Chad is a returned missionary!"

Upstairs, Brian was giving directions like the scarecrow in the Wizard of Oz, pointing one boy one way and the next another, trying to steer everyone toward the appropriate task. "That goes in the hamper," he said to one. "Brush your teeth, *now*," was his instruction to another.

As Erica and I joined the others, Brian whispered to me, "I'm going to become an Afghanistani Freedom Fighter."

I smiled. "Oh, you are?"

"Yes," he said. "They figure a man who has no freedom will fight the hardest."

"Good thinking." I caught one of the triplets coming out of the bathroom. "Go back and hang up your towel," I said.

That night, as Gizmo snored beside our bed, it was Brian who couldn't go to sleep. I had the privilege of hearing all the things I hadn't let him say to Erica.

"What kind of kid doesn't even say hello when he meets you?" Brian said. It was all rhetorical, so I just listened. "That shirt looks like something Satan would wear," he went on. "And did you see how he stared at Erica? I'm burning those leotards. This is the end of ballet. Period! She can play hockey or something that involves a less-clingy uniform."

"Hockey?"

"That kid is bad news," Brian said. "I feel it in my gut."

I felt too much cake in mine, but I also shared Brian's awful suspicions.

"How much time does a person have to spend in the sun to get that kind of a tan, anyway?" Brian said. "His entire life? His hair is white, Andy. *White.*" I could almost feel Brian tensing up beside me. "He has a stringy-haired attitude, you know? He didn't make a single intelligent comment the entire evening. And Erica *likes* that guy! How can she like a kid like that? What could she possibly see in him?"

I yawned. "What's your point, dear?"

Brian just stared at me in astonishment, not in the mood for teasing.

I put a hand on Brian's arm. "Maybe she thinks guys on the edge are exciting. She's always been such a serious student; maybe someone like that seems adventurous or something."

"Adventurous?" Brian nearly shouted, as if I myself were defending the boy. "I'll tell you the kind of adventure a kid like that can offer. An adventure to juvenile court! Just look at that kid and tell me he doesn't take drugs."

"Maybe if you got up and paced, you'd feel better," I said.

Brian threw back the covers and sat up. "Why am I the only one who sees the emergency here? Why aren't you upset about this?"

"I am," I said. "It's just that weird thing we do, where one of us stays calm if the other one is hysterical. If I had been the one to panic, you'd be trying to calm me down."

Brian sighed. "Okay. Now it's your turn."

I laughed. "Look. I don't want her swooning over this kid either, but at least she can't date for another couple of years."

"Fifteen months," Brian corrected me. "If she's counting—

and she is—then *I'm* counting. And I'm screening every one of those little twerps, believe me."

I believed him. I could just picture Erica's dating years and the high blood pressure Brian would soon have. I remembered when Erica was two months old, and Brian was holding her in his arms as I got ready for bed one night. Just as I came into the bedroom to rock her and put her in her bassinet, I heard Brian say, ". . . so then Daddy blew up the busload of pimply teenage boys, and you lived at home with your Mommy and Daddy until you turned sixty. And then you went on your first date. The End."

Sure enough, Brian saw these boys as blips on his radar screen, enemy aircraft that must be eliminated before they capture Princess Erica. It was the father's version of a video game.

The next morning, as I knew he would, Brian chose to be a bit more subtle. For years we'd been studying the scriptures as a family at breakfast time. Brian and I felt this was the best send-off we could give our kids each day, and often we used it to teach timely lessons as specific needs arose.

Brian ignored yesterday's cliff-hanger starring the wicked king Noah, who was about to get fried by his own men, and instead taught a lesson on temple marriage. "Remember," he concluded, looking right at Erica, "you want to choose a mate you can be sealed to forever. Someone with the same commitment to the gospel that you have. Someone smart, considerate, ambitious, and hard-working. Someone who has high moral standards."

Erica smiled and finished off her orange juice. The older three then dashed off to collect their books as Brian and I sighed in relief.

"I think she's listening," Brian said.

I hugged him. "I know she is."

We all gathered by the front door to await Ryan, who was undoubtedly distracted by his belt, shoes or possibly a comb this time, and Erica said to Brian, "Dad, when did you know you were in love with Mom?"

Brian's eyes smiled as he thought. "Well," he said, trying

to pinpoint the exact moment, "I think it was when I came to pick your mom up for a date one time, and I met her cat."

Gizmo, back to his old self, trotted off to his favorite chair, uninterested in any story about cats.

Erica's eyebrows raised. "Her cat?"

"Yeah," Brian grinned, completely lost in his reverie. "She had this cat . . . named Irregardless."

"And then what?" Grayson asked.

Brian clicked back to the present. "That's when," he said.

Erica wrinkled her nose. Obviously not one of them understood the joke. "You fell in love with her because she had a cat?"

Brian chuckled. "No. Because of what she named him. I decided right then I had to marry that girl."

Ryan had joined us in the middle of Brian's recollection, and now all three of them were standing there, squinting, as if their parents were the biggest nerds in the world.

"I thought you said we should pick someone because they had all these, like, great qualities," Erica huffed. Then, as the kids jogged out to the van, she mumbled, "But I guess love conquers all."

Brian gulped as he watched his entire breakfast message fizzle into thin air. "Done in by my own example," he groaned.

I kissed him. "You're the most wonderful, romantic man I know," I said. "Thank you for falling in love with me."

Brian shrugged as he went out to drive the kids to school. "Couldn't be helped," he smiled.

That afternoon as I came back from grocery shopping, I noticed Brian's car in the garage. Since Brian never missed a day of teaching, I figured he must be terribly ill. I dashed right in to see if he was all right. "Brian?" I called. I glanced into the living room and saw him sitting in a chair, just staring straight ahead.

"Andy," he mumbled, his voice heavy with pain. "I've lost my job."

"What!" I threw my arms around him and listened in complete shock as Brian explained that nine professors had been laid off due to budget cutbacks. Last year eleven others had lost their jobs, and we had worried then that Brian would get swept up in the net. But after that dust had settled, the other professors were assured that their positions were secure.

"It just can't be," I said. I felt myself sinking into disbelief and rage, that such a terrible blow could come to our family. Brian and I cried together, then knelt in prayer.

"We have to exercise our faith in the Lord," Brian said, his voice choked with emotion. "He will watch over us."

I nodded, trying to grasp the situation and find enough strength to present a confident front for the children. The kids were unable to grasp the severity of the situation when we explained it to them. They just knew that Mom and Dad would make everything all right, and perhaps their naive responses were a good thing. Having the children worry wouldn't accomplish anything.

At the university, students picketed for a week to get classes reinstated, but the money simply wasn't there. Friends and relatives offered sympathy and meals, but we had to find a permanent solution. We were so grateful that we had followed the Church's plan to store food and build our savings. But even that couldn't last forever, and Brian immediately applied for work at other universities. Even so, the prospects looked bleak; universities across the country were cutting back, and history was one of the first departments to go.

"I guess Erica has her wish now," Brian said one night as we climbed into bed. "I no longer have an uncool job."

I smiled; finally Brian's sense of humor was returning. Everything would be all right.

I set the alarm clock. "I talked to Edith today. She said maybe this will be a blessing in disguise."

Brian chuckled at Edith's eternal optimism, then quoted Winston Churchill. "If so," he said, "the disguise is perfect."

CHAPTER 17

THE CALL OF THE FRUGAL BUGLE

Within a year, I had become a professional bag lady. That is, I could find more uses for a plastic trash bag than most people do for baking soda. Black bags covered the ground around the crops in our now-serious garden. With a hole in the top, they served as barber smocks as I saved hundreds of dollars by cutting the boys' hair myself. They served as painting tarps. They lined rain boots. They became Halloween spider costumes. They were cut into kites. They were slipped over hangers and used as garment bags. They kept dust off the computer and VCR. And, of course, they served as constant reminders to the children to keep their rooms clean.

Truly, I had become the provident woman. There was no bargain, no warehouse outlet, no discount dive that escaped my antennae. Any fool can walk in and pay retail, I thought to myself, delighted at the hundreds of dollars I was brilliantly saving by shopping in little-known alleys and back rooms. I felt like a genius, beating the system.

Brian's unemployment had not only taught us the difference between wants and needs, but it had made savers and recyclers of us all. I even used stray socks to make puppets, then when those wore out, they became dusting mittens. One of our neighbors finally asked me how I had so little garbage each week, when I had six children. "We use everything at least three times," I shrugged. Four, if you counted the compost pile.

Christmas gifts were strictly handmade, or were services printed on a coupon. I was amazed at the skills I had learned at homemaking meetings. Without even stopping to realize it, I had become almost as self-sufficient as Edith Horvitz. I was drying and canning fruit, sewing, making my own household cleaners, painting old shoes to look like new, gardening, upholstering, wallpapering, even doing small plumbing and electrical repairs.

Brian had used his extra time to learn how to fix everything else in the house, instead of hiring expensive workmen. It seemed he was constantly wiring, hammering and plastering. Our yard was a weed-free showcase, thanks to Brian's hours of toil and his efficient watering drip system. He even routed the tubes through huge water tanks which were attached to the back of the house for our water storage, constantly flushing fresh water through.

Junk food vanished. Books and videotapes were borrowed free from the library. Erica and I stopped buying the cosmetics, accessories, and jewelry that we thought we couldn't live without before. Even the little ones learned to appreciate the toys they had, instead of asking for every new one they heard about.

But despite the satisfaction that comes with learning self-sufficiency, we had emotional lessons to learn, too. Brian and I tried harder than ever to avoid quarreling, knowing that this financial strain was creating a perfect field for battle. In the process, we discovered ways to avoid arguments that we might never have considered before.

Our first move, whenever a quarrel began brewing, was to immediately kneel together in prayer. This softened—if not completely solved—most of our disputes. Other techniques included taking the "me" out—really recognizing selfishness and taking that out of the discussion. We also tried to disagree on paper sometimes, writing down all our arguments and then comparing our lists instead of shouting back and forth.

Another idea that helped us was to remember that if one half of the couple wins, you both lose. We really took seriously the idea that when we married we formed a solid unit. For half of that unit to fail would mean a failure for the whole. Real love cannot rejoice in the defeat of your spouse.

And finally, sometimes we simply gave in. We decided that the issue was not important enough to warrant bringing contention into our home. If our home was to be our family's temple, then it didn't make sense to fill that temple with harsh words or accusations. Having the courage to apologize—even when part of us wanted to prove we were right—brought great peace into our home. Our egos shrank to the appropriate size, and the fit was more comfortable for everyone.

Our testimonies grew, too. Through meeting adversity and relying upon the Lord, we were amazed at how our faith blossomed. We searched the scriptures far more deeply. Our prayers and fasting became more fervent and meaningful. After doing all we could, we then exercised faith and truly felt a constant, abiding closeness with the Holy Ghost. It was like joining a winning team; there was an unmistakable surge of confidence and inner peace.

But our struggle wasn't without its thorns. One day I went to the mall to buy a sweater for Erica's birthday, and as I sat in the parking lot trying to think of a store I could afford to shop in, I realized there wasn't one. I must have cried for fifteen minutes. I remember finally shaking myself mentally and thinking, "This is ridiculous, Andy. This is the pride that brought down nations in the Book of Mormon. Buying the latest fashions is not that important." But it still hurt, and some days it was simply harder to fight discouragement than on others.

Brian was coming out of a 7-11 one afternoon and a beggar sitting on the sidewalk asked him for spare change. "Hey, I've been out of work for a year myself," Brian barked, feeling more than his share of self-pity.

"Well, I've been out of work for two," the beggar said.

Brian was fed up with his life at that point and shouted, "You win!" as he got in the car. Immediately, he felt like a complete fool. The next day he drove back, saw the same fellow, and promised him a donation if he got work first.

"Yeah, sure," the beggar sneered. Now Brian felt sillier than ever.

Then one night during a family home evening, Cameron,

who had chosen wrestling with Brian for the activity that night, suddenly sat up straight and said, "Did anybody feel that earthquake?"

Erica and I had been in the kitchen (*somebody* has to be ice monitor during these wrestling sessions that always injure at least two people), but now we stuck our heads into the family room and listened. Nothing was rumbling or shaking. "I doubt you'd even notice one," I said, "you guys are so rowdy in there."

"Uh-oh," Brian said, focusing on the baseboards of one wall. "Have you noticed that crack before?"

I followed his stare to a half-inch separation between the wall and the floor. "How did that happen?" I asked.

We turned on the news but there were no reports of earthquakes. "I knew one day they'd break through the floor," Erica muttered.

The next day Brian asked Vern Emmett, a retired contractor in the ward, to come and look at the wall. "Can I go around back?" Brother Emmett asked. We opened the sliding door and he looked around. "Is there any access under your floor there?"

We showed him a trap door in the guest closet, which led to a crawl space under the raised foundation. Brother Emmett dropped down onto the ground and disappeared. Soon he was back up, brushing himself off and shaking his head. "Dunno how they got this past inspection," he said, "but those things happen. You've got no vents."

Brian and I looked at each other, then back at Brother Emmett. "So?"

"Your house was illegally built," he said. "You've got to have vents so moisture can evaporate. If you don't, you get dry rot. All your wood is crumbling and your whole floor is gonna give way."

"What!" Brian and I said in unison.

"That wood's soft as powder," Brother Emmett said.

"Can it be fixed?" I asked.

"Sure," he said, adjusting his baseball cap. "Get yourself some estimates. That's too big a job for me."

"Wh-wh-what are you thinking it will run?" Brian stuttered, his mouth dry.

Brother Emmett shrugged. "Well, they'll either have to tear up the entire bottom floor, or jack the house up and replace the bad wood. I'd say fifty thousand, these days."

Brian and I nearly fainted. Weakly, we thanked Brother Emmett and sat down in shock. "We can't afford that," I said, stating the obvious. "We'll lose our house."

"And we can't afford to let it fall through, either," Brian said.

We called our realtor the next day to see if the builder could be held responsible, but discovered that by signing a termite report, we had acknowledged knowing about the lack of ventilation, and the problem was our responsibility.

"But nobody ever said that having no vents means your house will collapse!" Brian said.

I thought of Edith's particle board house, and wondered if this was the same thing that had happened to her.

Brian paced the floor, then realized he was literally stomping on thin ice. He stopped in his tracks. "I've got to get work!" he shouted, ready to tear the house down himself.

"Maybe it's time I got a job," I said. We had talked about this months ago, and decided that the triplets still needed so much time that we'd wait until we were absolutely desperate before I'd go back to work. But with our food storage almost gone, and the prospect of losing our home, this felt pretty desperate. "Half the mothers in this country work full time," I said, "and another fourteen per cent work part time."

Brian sighed. "Have we caught up to Job yet?"

I hugged him. Unemployment was high, especially for former teachers such as myself, but I was willing to do anything. "Maybe I could substitute," I said.

"Do you know how many people are trying to do the same thing?" Brian said. "They won't even hire me! I'm going to see a head hunter this week, to see if he can find me something outside the field of teaching. Let's wait and see what happens, and if I still can't get hired somewhere—" he shrugged.

That afternoon Ryan got his braces off, a commitment we

had made before Brian was laid off. He came home grinning through a brand new retainer. "And you thought he couldn't be retained," I said to Brian, slipping the orthodontist's bill under a stack of mail for him to discover another day than today.

That night we had promised the children take-out burgers to celebrate Ryan's end to braces, and despite the day's bad news, Brian wanted to keep his word. The kids all clamored into Burger King as if it were the Ritz Carlton.

Brian's forehead broke out in tiny beads of sweat as he looked up at the menu and mentally calculated the dent this would place in our floor-repair budget. I squeezed his hand. "It's just one time," I whispered.

We waited behind a woman who finally got her order and was just walking away as Austin said, "That lady smelled awful!"

"Shh!" I said.

"Who?" Cameron asked. "That fat one?"

"The one with the mustache," Bennett answered.

The woman turned around and glared at our family. I wanted to crawl under the tiles.

"I want two Whoppers," Grayson announced.

"Me too," Ryan said.

"Do you have discounts on quantity orders?" Brian whispered to the kid behind the counter. But his question was lost in the noise.

"What?" the kid asked. Someone else began giving him their order, and Bennett tugged on Brian's hand.

"I want chicken!" Bennett screamed, to be heard above the din.

"Me too!" Austin and Cameron echoed.

Then one of the kids said something about a chocolate malt and a large order of fries. Another one started shouting about onion rings and Erica was specifying which salad she wanted. Ryan began arguing with Grayson about popcorn, and Brian went berserk. "That's it! Out of here!" he shrieked, raising his hands in defeat and pulling the children out of the restaurant. "You kids have no concept of the value of a dol-

lar! You think money grows on trees! We can't take you anywhere! You all go crazy!"

They stood like a row of obedient little von Trapps, cower-
ing outside the door. Even hyperactive Ryan was motionless.

"Brian," I said, taking his arm, "could I speak with you
privately for a moment?" This was the cue we had agreed
upon to challenge a parenting decision without doing so in
front of the kids.

Brian's head was still jerking around as I yanked him into
the restaurant again. "You are losing it at a Burger King," I
hissed. "Get a grip!"

Brian waved his arms defensively. "What—the kids are
the ones—"

"The kids are just being kids," I said. "You are being Scrooge
McDuck. Now knock it off."

"Hey, I am a man with a mission," Brian said.

"You're a man with an omission," I said. "We'll find a way
to pay for the family room, but tonight isn't going to make or
break us."

Brian glanced back outside at our glum little group. "You're
right," he said. "I'm sorry."

I hugged him, then pinched his side as we headed back
out. "At least I don't have to worry about you going through a
second childhood," I said. "You're not through with your first
one."

CHAPTER 18

HAVE I GOT A JOB FOR YOU

Brian came home furious from his interview with the head hunter. "They gave me a test!" he exploded. "A psychological profile!"

I came around the corner wiping my hands on a dish towel. "Well, I'm sure you did fine, honey. You'll see."

"They graded it while I sat there," he snarled. "And they said I can't take criticism! Can you believe that? These people must be lunatics! Imagine saying *I* can't take criticism! That has to be the most ridiculous accusation I've ever heard. I am *fantastic* at taking criticism."

I tightened my cheek muscles so I wouldn't laugh and reminded myself that this was serious.

"What do you think about that?" Brian went on.

"Oh, I agree completely," I said.

Brian seemed satisfied and headed up to the bedroom to take off his tie. I was glad I didn't have to clarify with whom I agreed.

Brian came down with the stack of papers listing the universities where he had applied to teach. "There's got to be another one I can contact," he said, spreading them out on the dining room table.

"Here's one in Canada," I said, pointing to the listing of a city where, according to Ryan's recent report on polar bears, the most deaths by bear attack occur.

"Forget it," Brian said. "That's an entire town participating in a cryogenics experiment. Top summertime temperature is forty something."

"But maybe we need to go somewhere where the Church can be built up."

"I'm all for that," Brian said. "I figure wherever we go it will be for the punishment of the community. I mean the betterment."

I laughed. "You've been hanging around Edith."

"I did talk with her today, as a matter of fact," Brian said. "She offered me a job."

I smiled and tried to imagine what it could be. Cataloging her crochet patterns? Being a guinea pig in her science lab?

"She wants me to manage Edith Enterprises," Brian continued. "She says it's grown too big for her to handle alone."

"That would be great!" I exclaimed.

Brian closed his eyes and held the bridge of his nose. "Andy, you must be on drugs."

"What's wrong with running Edith's company?"

Brian stared at me as if I were crazier than Edith. "Don't you realize who we're talking about, here? This is a woman who has been hospitalized for insanity, Andy. This is a totally deranged person—a woman who glued a toupee on my head and caused me to get scalped when we were in London."

"Oh, that," I said.

"'Oh, that'?" Brian mocked. "Excuse me, but I think that alone is reason enough for me to stay as far away from Edith Horvitz as possible."

"You're nursing a grudge," I said. "Edith's on some kind of medication that is doing absolute wonders for her. Besides, I think you'd have fun working for Edith."

Brian was almost speechless, and squeaked as he tried to respond. "Fun? You call a woman fun who squirts glue onto people's heads? You think it's fun when she tells people about eating birdseed to avoid constipation?" Brian was waving his hands, his eyes wild with emotion. "You think her macaw is fun? Was it fun when she served those terrible bone things at Nick's wedding? Was it fun when she baby-sat the triplets and we came home to find them stuck to a Velcro wall?"

I smiled, recalling what Edith had done last year when we asked to her baby-sit in an emergency. She had dressed the boys in fuzzy jackets and tossed them onto a huge sheet of Velcro that she'd tacked onto one of our walls. "All happy, all in one place," she bragged when we got home. We were horrified until we realized that the kids were laughing and having the time of their lives and didn't want to come down. Even Ryan and Grayson later complained that they hadn't gotten to try it.

"You think I'd work for a madwoman like that?" Brian said. "I'd be locked up myself in two weeks."

I laughed. "Okay, okay," I said. "But it was a sweet offer."

Brian shook his head. "Sweet," he muttered under his breath. "And you let the kids call her 'Aunt Edith.' Ha!"

Nick and Zan, our only well-fixed relatives, had offered to help, and while we were grateful for the many times they took the kids on excursions we couldn't possibly have afforded, we couldn't allow them to support us.

Paula and Mike were always dodging creditors of their own, so they were the last people we would turn to.

Natalie's husband, Gorman, had offered to lend us money once or twice. But he had his hands full with Chad. Our suspicions turned out to be not only right, but underestimates. Chad, who threw Natalie into a stupor by moving in with them, was stealing to support a drug habit, and was driving his dad to the poorhouse in the fast lane. He had blazed a trail through every detoxification house in the area, and Gorman was now looking into special schools that lock kids up until they graduate high school.

Fortunately, while Erica still liked guys who lived on the edge, she drew the line at guys who were *over* the edge, and Chad was definitely that.

Natalie, of course, was thrown into the deep end of the parenting pool. For a woman who never wanted the responsibility of children, Natalie had certainly signed up for a full bushel.

And our mothers were both living on limited incomes, so despite wanting to bail us out of our problems, there wasn't much they could do to help.

That night as Brian and I headed upstairs to bed, I said,

"You know, it's such a shame. Over the years we have mastered a number of talents, not one of which pays a thing."

"Such as?"

I stopped him on the landing to tell him my list. "Well, fluency in Pig Latin, for example."

"A good one," Brian agreed.

"Tongue curling," I continued, "saying the alphabet backwards, diapering babies in record time. Picking up objects with our toes. And I believe you have perfect pitch."

"One of us is also an expert at keeping people from going to bed at night."

"I am not," I said, pretending to be miffed, and shoving Brian playfully in the chest. But Brian lost his footing and stumbled down the stairs.

"Oh, sure," he shouted. "Try to kill me. Go for the policy." Luckily, he landed on his feet.

I stood on the landing, laughing, with my hands on my hips. "That was an accident and you know it. You are such a brat."

The next morning Edith came over and said she wasn't going to take no for an answer. She wanted Brian to manage EE, and that was final. Brian was still upstairs, so I told her I'd go and get him.

"Forget it," Brian said, rinsing his face off after shaving. "Besides, how do you pronounce 'EE'? Isn't that the sound a mouse makes? What if Edith hires a receptionist? How will she answer the phone—'*Eeee?*'" Brian dried his face and put on a shirt. "People will think they've reached a broken answering machine," he said.

I smiled as I pulled Brian to the stairs. "Brian, she did win the Nobel prize."

Brian pretended to be impressed. "And I hear she also has a hit record!" He buckled his belt and said, "We'd have to be in a dire emergency for me to consider working with Edith."

I stopped and stared at him. He'd been out of work for over a year, we were running out of food and money, and our floor was caving in. "Well, maybe one will come up," I said.

Brian scowled.

"Come on," I said. "At least be courteous."

Brian followed me down to where Edith was waiting. "Hello, Edith," he said, his voice tight with irritation. We sat down.

"Brian Taylor," she said, "I need you to manage Edith Enterprises. I'm dead serious. You have a good head on your shoulders."

"Yes," Brian started in, "one that you once tried to cover with—"

"Brian," I interrupted, "Let's let Edith finish what she has to say."

Edith smiled. "I need a sharp guy like you to run the business end of things, so I can work on my experiments."

"Why don't you ask Nick?" Brian said. "That's right down his alley."

"Nick's already head poncho for that pharmaceutical company," Edith said. I tried to picture such an item of apparel. "Besides," Edith continued, "Nick doesn't have your expertise."

Brian laughed. "What expertise? I'm not a businessman, Edith. I'm a history professor."

Edith raised her pointer finger, delighted. "That's right! See, most folks would hire an accountant or a businessman, but not me. No-o-o sir! I want an advisor. A guy who knows trends. I'm not just in this for my health, y'know."

We smiled.

Edith leaned forward. "What's the best predictor of the future?"

Brian sighed. "The past."

"Exactly," Edith said, as if tutoring him. "So a historian is the best person to forecast what inventions are gonna be hot."

"Well, thanks for dropping by," Brian said, getting to his feet and reaching out to shake her hand.

Edith stood up and pushed him back down onto the sofa. "Look here," she said, "I may be crazy, but I'm not stupid!"

We paused to let that one sink in, and Edith continued. "You know every invention and when it was invented and what it did to society," she said. "You know what's ahead for the human race because everything's a cycle. Right?"

Brian smiled. This happened to be one of his pet theories, largely substantiated by the cycles of prosperity, pride, destruction, then repentance, in the Book of Mormon.

"I'm not saying you can predict the weather a week from Tuesday," Edith said, "or who's gonna win some ball game. I'm talking about global stuff. What gadgets they're gonna need in foreign countries, based on where their politics are goin'."

Brian was still smiling. "I understand what you're saying," he said, "and I'm flattered that you think I could do all that. But I just don't think *anyone* can pinpoint the inventions that we'll be needing in the future."

"You may be right," Edith said, standing over him. "But you may be wrong, too. And I like to hedge my bets. So *in case* it can be done, I want to hire a history expert, not a numbers guy. Numbers I can get on my calculator."

Brian laughed. "Edith, you're talking about managing a business, not sitting around with a crystal ball—"

"You had a double major in college," Edith said. "History and math."

Brian's jaw dropped. "How did you know that?"

Edith rolled her eyes. "You think I'd hire you without checking this stuff out? You got good grades, too."

"Edith!" Brian was incensed that she would pry into his past like that.

Edith just stood there, self-satisfied, and went on. "Hey, we both know you can handle the business side of it," she said. "What—am I supposed to think *Andy* pays the bills? Ha!" She snorted at the absurdity of such an idea.

I opened my mouth to retort, but couldn't think of a good one.

"So," Edith said, patting Brian on his head, "I'd say you got it all, Brian. You can handle the books, plus you can see the big picture. Maybe," Edith wiggled her pencil-thin eyebrows, "even the future."

"No, no," Brian said. "You're asking the wrong guy."

Edith smiled and turned to leave. "It could be temporary—

just until you get hired by another university. Think about it," she said. "Oh, there is one small catch," she added (as if working with Edith Horvitz was not a giant catch all by itself). "I just inherited my aunt's old house. She's been in a convalescent home for years, and finally kicked the ol' bucket. So she willed me her place over on Brentmore. I'm moving in this weekend, but it's too big a place for me to live in alone. So I want my manager—and his family, of course—to live there, too. Everything under one roof."

"What!" I gasped. "You want us to move in with you?" This was so far over the limit it wasn't even funny.

Edith looked surprised at *my* surprise. "Well," she shrugged, "it's a big house. Has a couple of wings, a library. Each of your kids could have his own room. You've probably seen the place. It's between Pembrooke and White Creek."

Brian and I stared at each other in shock as Edith said, "Well, you folks think it over. I'll be in touch."

Then she drove off.

"Is she serious?" Brian whispered. "She just inherited the Drossett mansion?"

I shook my head. "That's impossible!"

"That place looks like the Pentagon, for crying out loud," Brian said. "Well, mansion or not, I couldn't live—or work—with Edith Horvitz."

"On the other hand," I said, "You already know how she is."

"That's the good news *and* the bad news," Brian said. "No, positively not. I won't even consider it."

I nodded. He was a history professor. Managing Edith Enterprises was simply out of the question.

"How did she know about my cycles theory?" Brian asked during dinner that night.

"I doubt she did," I said. "She just probably has the same philosophy."

Brian almost choked at the idea of sharing a thought with Edith Horvitz.

"What theory?" Grayson asked.

"Oh, Aunt Edith came by today," I said, watching from the corner of my eye as Brian grimaced on the word *aunt*.

"Ant Eater! Ant Eater!" the triplets chanted, happily banging their forks on the table.

"She wants us to move into the Drossett Mansion with her," I said casually.

"That place on Brentmore?" Erica gasped. "How is she moving into that?"

"It seems she inherited it, but that's just a rumor," Brian said, trying to catch my eye so he could glare at me. "Pass the salad, please."

"Wow," Erica said. "That place is huge."

"She wants Daddy to work for her," I said.

"All right!" Ryan and Grayson shouted in unison.

"Ant Eater! Ant Eater!" the triplets began chanting again.

Erica's face lit up. "You would be working for Edith Horvitz? Oh, cool!"

Steam was almost coming out of Brian's ears now, as he stared daggers in my direction.

"It would be neat for Dad to work for a Nobel prize winner, huh?" I said to Erica.

"Well, yeah, but I was thinking how cool to work for a rock star," Erica said. "I heard one of her rap songs yesterday at Shanell's house. It was pretty cool." Edith had kept her word, and had recently recorded her albums of hits from the eighties *and* the nineties.

Now I turned to wink at Brian and mouthed, "Cool!"

"And since our floor is sinking anyway . . ." Grayson said.

"Well, your mother is only teasing," Brian said. "It's completely ridiculous to consider moving in with Sister Horvitz."

We all stared at him, waiting for the reasons why.

"Come on, everybody!" Brian spat the words out like hot soup. "Don't you realize"—he struggled to find the right words, not wanting to say Edith was nuts in front of the children, who adored her—"that it simply couldn't work?"

"Why not?" Ryan asked.

"Stop tapping your fork, honey," I said, resting my hand on his ever-moving wrist. We all waited for the answer.

Brian's head jerked around as he looked for one of us to side with him. "People don't just move in together!" he said.

"People need privacy. There." Brian smiled, sure he had settled the matter.

"But we'd have even more in that big place!" Grayson said. "We could each have our own bedrooms *and* our own bathrooms."

That was the magic word for Erica. "Oh, please, Daddy, please-oh-please! We've got to move in with Aunt Edith!"

"We'd probably never even bump into her," I said, avoiding eye contact with Brian, who I knew was ready to clobber me. "And if you worked for her, you wouldn't have to drive anywhere!"

"Yeah!" Grayson said. "Talk about a fast commute!"

Brian's nostrils flared and his lips were curling. "And what about her macaw?"

We all considered that for a moment. "Well, it would probably stay in her bedroom," I offered.

Erica brightened. "Or maybe it will have a room of its own!"

"It isn't even within our ward boundaries," Brian said. "There."

I shrugged. "We'd have to change wards, then."

"We can't move until the floor is fixed," Brian said. "You can't sell a broken house. There."

"We could fix it after we save up enough money. Then we could sell it," I suggested.

Brian was gripping his knife and fork with white knuckles. "Look. We are not doing this. Is that clear? I don't care if the house falls in. We are not moving in with Sister Horvitz and that's final."

CHAPTER 19

LETTING EDITH'S LIGHT SHINE

The day we moved our last belongings over to the Drossett Mansion—now EE Headquarters—Edith strung a big banner out front, reading: WELCOME HOME TAILORS!

"Good grief," Brian muttered as we pulled through huge iron gates and onto the massive driveway. "It looks like somebody's been living here in ill-fitting clothes."

I laughed and squeezed his arm. "I'm so happy," I said. "This really was a blessing in disguise, wasn't it?"

Brian sighed. "I'm reserving judgment." Brian had remained adamantly opposed to this move for at least a week after Edith had approached him (and even more adamantly opposed to my recruiting the kids to campaign with me). But the realization that our home was downright dangerous, and that we simply had to move out as quickly as possible, helped convince Brian to fast and pray about it with an open mind.

"Semi-open," he'd conceded.

Finally, after rising from his knees one night, he sat on the bed for a minute, deep in concentration. Then he fell back onto his pillow, staring straight up at the ceiling. "I can't believe it," he croaked, his voice almost wincing with pain. "We're moving in with Edith!"

I had already climbed into bed, having received my own answer during Edith's visit, and now I threw my arms around him.

"Oh, honey, this will be wonderful! You'll see," I said, almost crying with joy.

"Why is the Lord giving me this test?" Brian moaned.

"Wasn't it enough that we've been unemployed for sixteen months? Or that our house is falling in? And now he's inflicting Edith Horvitz on me!"

I laughed. "Don't you see the blessing in this? Now we'll have a free place to stay while we raise the money to fix the floor. How could we have done it if you'd been hired by another university? We couldn't have sold the house like it is, and we'd have lost it. Then, we'd have had nothing to put down on a new one."

Brian's voice was almost a squeak. "But Edith Horvitz . . ."

"You'll be the perfect balance for Edith," I told him. "You're so practical and sensible."

Brian had held his hands over his face. "Oh, no," he wailed softly. "I'm the rudder for Edith Horvitz's speedboat!"

I kindly resisted the urge to mention a dinghy.

And now, here we were, moving into her huge estate, the kids running up and down the spacious halls and screaming, "Yahoo! Hey, where am I?" as they literally got lost among its endless corridors. Thank goodness most of the doors on the third floor were locked, or we might never have found our children.

"Brian!" Edith shouted, sticking her goggled head out of an office near the entry. "First item of business. Let's call the queen of England and invite her over here to see *our* Buckingham Palace!"

Brian's shoulders hunched up around his ears as his muscles cramped around that thought.

"Oh, sorry!" Edith shouted, noting Brian's stiff posture. "I guess you should check the books first and see if that sort of thing's in our budget."

Brian nodded and lowered his shoulders. "Remember," he whispered to me after Edith had disappeared, "this is only until I'm offered a teaching position."

Painters were crossing paths with movers that day, as Edith went ahead with her plans to spruce up the neglected exterior. As they splashed on ivory paint, movers and members of the elders' quorum hauled in our tables and beds, lamps and dishes.

Edith had given us the entire left side of the massive home, and used part of her own quarters for her science lab and business office. Angel did indeed have his own room, painted in a jungle mural, complete with a sun-room attached.

"I think moving in with Edith will be a good thing for Andy," my mother had whispered to Brian. "Edith's so stable; I think she'll be a good influence. You know, ever since Andy attacked those balloons . . ."

"Great," I said to Brian when he relayed my mom's sentiments. "Edith and I have officially switched places."

The older kids began ripping open their boxes and pulling out their belongings as if they'd been missing these treasures for weeks. Eagerly they filled their closets and shelves, while I helped the triplets move into their own rooms.

Soon I heard sniffling coming from Bennett's room. He and Cameron were standing there, arms around each other, crying. "What's the matter?" I asked, kneeling down to wipe their tears.

"I don't want to be alone," Bennett said.

"Me neither," Cameron sniffled.

Austin, who had walked in with me, had tears in his eyes as well. "Can't we stay in the same room, Mom?"

I sighed and held all three of them in a giant hug. "Of course you can. You don't *have* to have your own rooms." The triplets cheered.

Ryan, passing by, shook his head in disbelief and kept on walking.

Brian and I rearranged the triplets' quarters so they could still be together. I had noticed for a couple of years now that the triplets really cherished one another. I saw a tremendous amount of empathy between them, a bond of loyalty I only wished I could foster among *all* the children.

Usually when siblings have a disagreement, parents intervene to protect the weaker one. But with siblings who are the same age, we found that they really were capable of working things out fairly among themselves. By not intervening as much, we had inadvertently taught them to get along better.

Members of our new Relief Society arrived with casseroles

and scrumptious dishes for dinner, then helped us unpack.
Members from our former ward, too, were on hand to wish us
well and let us know we were still in their hearts. We felt
caressed by their love and gently handed over to our new
ward family.

Brian slipped out in the late afternoon and drove to the old
7-11, where he found the beggar he had spoken to weeks
before. "Could you use ten dollars?" Brian asked him.

The fellow's eyes lit up like Christmas lights. "I sure could!"
he said. "God bless you!"

"I got a job," Brian said, by way of explanation.

But there was no recognition in the man's eyes; to Brian's
relief, the man had obviously forgotten all about their earlier
encounter.

That night we all sank into our beds, exhausted after the
big move. But Ryan, still the last to nod off, came charging into
our room at eleven-thirty.

"Mom! Dad! Wake up! You gotta see this!"

Brian and I were startled from our sleep and jumped up as
if a fire alarm had sounded. "What? What?"

"Come on!" Ryan said, pulling us down the hall and roust-
ing the rest of the family as he went.

"What's going on?" Erica asked, throwing on a robe and running behind us.

"Come on, you guys," Ryan called into the triplets' room.

"Let them sleep," I said, pulling Ryan away. "What's this
all about?"

Ryan dragged us out the door, down the steps and out onto
the front lawn. Then he turned us around to face the house.
"Look!" he shouted.

Grayson's mouth fell open and he whispered, "Awesome!"

Brian's and my eyes froze open.

Erica said, "I have never been so embarrassed in my whole
life."

Brian swallowed. "It glows," he croaked, his voice laden
with woe. "The entire house *glows.*" Sure enough, Edith had
covered the house with glow-in-the-dark paint.

"I don't believe this," I mumbled.

"Me either!" Grayson reveled, as if beholding the eighth wonder of the world. He and Ryan gave each other high fives. "So cool!" I heard one of them say.

"I can't live here," Erica whimpered. "How could she do this?"

I sighed. If she had used mood paint instead, the house would be a crazy quilt of joy, humiliation and pure exasperation.

I put an arm around Erica and thought to myself, we look like the people you see on the evening news, standing there in their nightgowns, watching their home burn down.

"Click your heels, everybody," Brian said, "and say, 'There's no place like home.' Maybe it will work."

Staring at the pale greenish glow on all our faces, I too longed for our old house with its sinking floor.

Brian walked back into the house with Erica, shaking his head and muttering, "Just a bad dream, just a bad dream."

I caught up to them and said, "It's not so bad, really. It looks cream-colored in the daylight. And anyway, who really drives by at night? Nobody."

"I can't wait to tell everyone at school," Grayson was saying, right on my heels.

Erica shuddered. "Oh, great! I'm going to die."

Just as we got to Ryan's room, Brian put one hand on our son's shoulder and said, "Thanks *so* much for waking us up for that inspiring experience."

An eclipse of the brain, I thought to myself.

The next day Ryan woke the triplets up, telling them all about the phosphorescent mansion, and the entire day they kept asking when it would be night so they could see it for themselves.

"Edith," Brian said as she joined us for the end of breakfast, "we noticed the paint job on the house—"

"I sure hope so!" Edith said. "Ain't it great? Sometimes I amaze even myself! I figure it'll save thousands of bucks a year on outdoor lighting. We won't even need a porch light!"

"That's for sure," I agreed.

"And," Edith went on, "what burglar will come within

twenty feet of this place if his every move is lit up? I'll bet you can see our house for a mile!" Edith cackled with joy, slapped Brian on the knee, grabbed a slice of toast and vanished down the hallway.

"Let's not push this," I said to Brian as the kids gathered up their school books. "I mean, Edith has really done a lot for us, and after all, it is her house—"

Brian sighed. "What about Erica?"

"I don't know," I said. "Maybe we can think of something."

But within a week, Erica, Grayson and Ryan had become the most popular kids on campus for living in "the Addams Family House."

"Think of the spook alleys we could have on Halloween!" Ryan said, slapping his backpack down on the dining table. Grayson's pals were begging to sleep over so they could see the glowing up close. And Erica, known for being prim and studious, had suddenly acquired a plucky reputation for living in such eccentric quarters. Now she was seen as mysterious—a chic trendsetter you'd expect to read about in some avant-garde teen magazine. Kids were admiring her for quirks that actually belonged to Edith Horvitz. Rumors were even spreading that Erica was related to Edith—a definite plus among teachers who admired Edith's Nobel prize, and among teenagers who admired Edith's ridiculous rock star image.

One morning the phone rang and Brian picked it up. "It's a member of the stake presidency," he whispered, his hand covering the receiver. "He wants to give you a calling."

Since moving from our old ward Brian had been called as Young Men's president, but I hadn't yet been given a new job. "What's the calling?" I whispered, my eyes dancing with anticipation as I moved towards Brian.

"It's a new position they just created," he whispered. "Stake Dresser of the Dead."

I froze in my tracks. "What?"

Brian shrugged, as stunned as I, and handed me the phone.

"Hello?" I squeaked, my voice as wobbly as my knees. This couldn't be happening to me! My worst fear was descending upon me like a blanket of cold slime.

"Hi, Sister Taylor," President Ferguson said. "You've been requested for a new calling. Could you meet with me this evening?"

"Wha-wha-what is it?" I stammered. "Is it d-d-dressing the d-d-dead?"

President Ferguson chuckled, and I spun around to look at Brian, who was doubled over and red-faced in stifled hysterics.

I shook my fist at Brian and quietly mouthed, "You are dead meat," as I made an idiotic and flustered explanation to President Ferguson that my husband is such a kidder.

I hung up and pounced on Brian. "How dare you scare the daylights out of me like that?" I yelled. "I could have had a heart attack!"

Brian was laughing so hard he was crying. As I pummeled him with my fists, he only laughed harder

"I'll dress the dead, all right," I snarled. "Starting with you!" He was so delighted with his joke that he was weak with glee. I gave him one last slug and stomped off.

That night President Ferguson asked me to serve as second counselor in the stake Relief Society presidency. My normal reaction would have been to tremble in the face of that much responsibility, but instead I sighed with relief. No calling in the Church seemed too formidable after Brian's little shenanigans.

Edith had been given a new calling, too, as nursery assistant. Any woman who would invite a family of six children to move in with her has to like kids, right?

Wrong. Actually, it wasn't so much that Edith didn't like them. It was just that she had never been around a lot of kids and didn't approach them in the traditional way. Come to think of it, Edith didn't approach anything in the traditional way, so maybe we should have expected what happened.

The second Sunday into her calling, a pizza delivery man came to the bishop's office asking for a Miss Horvitz in the nursery.

Bishop Weller, a very serious, rotund man who swayed from side to side as he marched down the halls, led the way to the nursery.

"Sister Horvitz," he said, his voice a staccato call to order, "did you order a pizza?"

Edith looked up from her toddlers, all of whom raised a cheer when they heard that their treat had arrived. "Perfect timing," she crowed, clapping her hands. "Just put it on the table here. Bishop, pull up a chair and join us. I brought root beer."

Passersby in the hallway remember this incident as the first time they'd ever seen Bishop Weller gasp and grope for words. "Bu-bu-but Sister Horvitz," he said.

"If you don't like pizza," Edith said, "you can just sit back and enjoy the show."

Bishop Weller turned at that moment and saw Binky the Clown in the corner, tying balloons into dachshunds and giraffes.

"What's the magic word?" Binky asked, in a voice like Woody Woodpecker's.

"Abracadabra!" the kids all yelled.

"That's right!" Binky then made a springy cluster of silk flowers appear in his white-gloved hand, and honked his red nose.

"Who is this?" Bishop Weller asked.

"Binky. Got him out of the yellow pages under party planning," Edith said.

Bishop Weller just blinked at the scene before him. As Edith described it, he then asked to speak with her privately and explained that the nursery is not supposed to order pizza and hire a party clown.

Edith snorted as she told it. "So there goes my inflatable Moon Bounce idea."

SCRAMBLED HOME EVENINGS

"Dog mints. The woman has sold her formula for dog mints," Brian said as he dug into his Chinese chicken salad. He had taken me out to lunch to celebrate paying off the floor repair in our old house. The remodel turned out to cost less than half what Brother Emmett had estimated, and was finished three weeks after the workmen began. At last we could put it on the market. It looked so beautiful; it was a shame we couldn't move back into it. But Edith was adamant: her business manager had to live on the premises.

Brian was still struggling to accept Edith's wild ideas, and was utterly astonished every time one of them hit. But he dutifully tallied up the profits and kept Edith Enterprises running in the black. Nevertheless, he let Edith know that he was still hoping to get back into teaching history.

"Whatever made her come up with dog mints?" I asked, envisioning breath-sweetened dogs trotting up and down the blocks of America's neighborhoods.

Brian blushed. "I think I did," he said.

I laughed. "You?"

"Well, I was griping about Gizmo's breath one day," he said. "I caught Austin brushing Gizmo's teeth—by the way, what color is your toothbrush?"

"Not funny," I said.

Brian went on. "It's hard to get used to someone who listens to every word I say."

I asked the waitress for another lemonade.

"I said it's hard to get used to someone who LISTENS TO EVERY WORD I SAY," Brian repeated.

"I'm sorry," I laughed. "Were you talking, honey?"

Brian gave me a glance. "Anyway, she filed away my comments about Gizmo, and coerced me into making some predictions."

"And you predicted that dog mints would be the next rage?" I could hardly contain my astonishment.

"All I did was point out a few trends. You have a lot of kids growing up without a lot of parenting," Brian said. "This breeds selfishness. Has to. Anyway, as they grow into adulthood, more and more of them choose to have pets instead of children. Children require too much sacrifice. And yet these same people adore their pets."

I pulled a pinch off my roll and buttered it as I listened.

"Another trend is to protect animals," Brian said. "There's a real upswing in people caring about endangered species and animal experimentation. There are several bills pending which increase animal rights. Pet cemeteries are doing a good business, and now some party companies even throw parties for pets."

"How does that lead to dog mints?"

Brian smiled. "Well, it's amazing. You plug two parts of an equation into Edith's mind, and out come these startling conclusions. Edith decided the time was right for people to give their dogs the gift of fresh breath."

"How did she get a dog to eat something that smells like mint?"

"Well, you know Edith and her scent experiments. Now she's developed one that even a dog's nose can't detect. She's made the thing smell like cheese or something, until it mixes with saliva. Then . . . viola! Mint. She tried it on Gizmo and he loved it."

I shook my head. If it could work on Gizmo, it could work on any one. I mean any dog.

"And," Brian said, "the owner of the dog food company who's going to market them is a big advocate of community clean-up. He heard about Edith's graffiti thing on the news and wanted to meet her."

I shook my head. Who would have thought? A month ago Edith had been on the national news because some college kid

with a video camera had caught her spraying a brick wall at
the local parks and recreation building.

At first, the kid thought he was catching a vandal spraying
graffiti all over the wall, which seemed to have been marked
by every gang member in Southern California who couldn't
spell properly. But as he watched through his lens, he saw that
this sixtyish woman was covering the graffiti with brick-col-
ored paint (her own invention). "Grandma to the rescue," he
chuckled on the sound track.

But, typical of Edith, rather than stop with the simple
cleaning up of the wall, Edith decided to prevent future graffiti. She climbed onto a little ladder she had brought along, and
wrote in bold black letters across the top of the wall: ALL IDIOTS
SIGN BELOW.

Well, as it played on the news, you could hear the cam-
eraman cracking up and cheering for this vigilante senior cit-
izen. And, after going back the next week, he was so delighted
to see that it had worked, that he sent his tape to the network
news.

Soon reporters discovered that this secret heroine was
none other than the Nobel prize winning, hit song singing, Day-
Glo mansion dwelling Edith Horvitz.

Now she was trying to invent a paint that no other paint
could stick to, so walls could be painted with it and never be
marred by graffiti again. Trust Edith.

She was never at a loss for a new idea. Last week Brian had
rushed into our wing, slammed the door and yelled, "That
does it! That does it! I cannot work for Edith Horvitz."

"Calm down, honey," I said, trying to angle him into a chair.

But Brian's back was like steel, and he wouldn't bend to sit
down. "Now she's trying to take over the world."

I sighed. I wanted so much to say, Oh, now, let's not exaggerate. But with Edith, anything was possible. I cleared my
throat. "How?"

Brian was pacing now, waving his arms. "She thinks she can
replace all the satellites with dolphins."

"Excuse me?"

"You heard me," Brian said, pacing. "Dolphins! She asked

me how much I knew about dolphins one day, and I said they swim and they're gray. That's the extent of my dolphin knowledge."

"And then?"

"And then she goes off without me, half-cocked as usual, and comes up with some crazy animal support group who'll back her in this plan of hers to do away with communications satellites!"

"Whoa," I said. "Back up and explain this." I tried to envision dolphin astronauts orbiting the earth.

"It's the way she thinks," Brian sputtered. "She turns things upside down, backwards, inside out. She said everybody is trying to communicate by beaming messages out into space, and bouncing them off satellites."

"So?"

"So she thinks it would be cheaper and smarter to go the other way—down. Into the ocean. She thinks dolphins can provide some vast underwater network for us. They're so helpful, intelligent, blah-blah-blah. Boy Scouts with fins, she says."

I smiled at the concept. Why not try it?

Brian whirled around. "You're smiling! Don't you smile! Do you think she would hesitate to build a giant dolphin tank in the house, and bring in a hundred dolphins? You think you wouldn't have to feed them and listen to them squeak?"

I stopped smiling.

"Aha!" Brian said. "Now you know what I go through every day. Every time that woman opens her mouth my heart pounds, because I know it's gonna be another crazy—and you can underline *crazy*—theory of hers."

"Did you tell her how upset you were?"

Now Brian slumped into a chair. "No," he said, disappointed in himself. "I told her I had to go take an Advil."

I laughed. "Well, I doubt one woman and a group of dolphin supporters could overthrow the entire space program."

"We are not talking about one woman," Brian sighed. "We are talking about Edith. Somehow, she counts extra."

Our family home evenings had now expanded to include Edith, of course, plus Nick's family since we'd moved from the ward and didn't see them as often, Natalie and Gorman now that they were a family and wanted to do things right, and my mother. Paula and Mike dropped in occasionally, and even Brian's mom stopped by if she was in town on a Monday. We encouraged the kids to invite their friends to join in, and by the time everyone arrived, we often had a bigger turnout than some ward dinners.

A friend of Ryan's, Joey Goldstein, had become a regular Monday guest and was even taking the missionary lessons. "My mom said I could," Joey said, "even though I think she's anesthetic."

Edith nodded; this kid spoke her language perfectly.

"You mean agnostic?" Brian asked.

"Yeah," Joey said, as he and the other kids broke up laughing. "But she likes that Mormons do their gerontology."

Again Edith nodded, and I had to look away to hide my grin.

"You mean genealogy," Grayson said.

"That's what he said," Edith jumped in. She and Joey were definitely kindred spirits. "Andy's got a great family tree," she went on. "Tell him about it, Andy."

I sighed. I had recently made a breakthrough in my English line, which had led to three convicts and a madam. Edith got hold of the information and had been dubbing it "rich stuff" ever since.

"Oh, you tell it better than I do," I said. So Edith gladly embellished my ancestors' escapades for our visitor.

Brian's mom, a nonmember, even consented to teach a lesson once, and threw all but Brian on their ears as part of a karate demonstration. Her Hawaiian boyfriend, the karate instructor at her retirement village, had obviously been tutoring Grandma Taylor.

"What a great lesson on self defense," I later told her.

"Self defense nothing," Grandma Taylor winked. "You folks couldn't defend yourselves out of a paper bag. That was a lesson on respecting your elders."

Paula refused to teach a lesson, claiming it would stress her out, and Mike nodded. "You don't want that to happen," he said, the true voice of experience. But occasionally she'd bring a gallon of ice cream, which the kids promptly inhaled.

One night Bennett taught a lesson, heavily aided by Erica, on the sacrament.

"The sacrament," Erica whispered into Bennett's ear.

"The sacrament," Bennett obediently repeated.

"Is a sacred ordinance," she whispered.

Bennett swallowed and solemnly said, "Is a secret ornament."

After one of Brian's lessons it was my turn to help the kids with a puppet show. We used a width of felt with a window cut in it, which we hung in a doorway for the puppet theater. "I need a tension rod," I said to Brian.

"First of all," he said, "you get more than enough attention. And second of all, my name's not Rod."

I smirked. "You're such a help. Why don't you tell your story about the fourth wise man, while I look for the tension rod?"

"*I'll* decide what's next," he insisted. "I'm going to tell the story about the fourth wise man."

I sighed. Last week I had suggested that Brian barbecue with one of the new marinades I'd found at the store, and he had said, "I'll decide how to cook the meat. I think I'll use one of those new marinades."

Nick's and Zan's gifted children were astounding one and all as they recited the Articles of Faith and read fluently from various books when they taught their lessons. Even their flannel-board figures had been carefully colored within the lines. Brian endured their brilliance with all the patience he could muster.

One evening Blair and Nolan took turns reading the story of Daniel in the lion's den, and asked the triplets to illustrate it on a chalkboard as they spoke. Well, the boys got a little carried away with the manes, and by the time Blair and Nolan turned around the entire chalkboard looked like a mass of scribbles. Blair and Nolan frowned; they probably hadn't scribbled since infancy.

Brian cleared his throat and announced to the crowd, "They're just not the same without their calligraphy pens."

That same evening Erica—for reasons still unclear to me—
had invited Jeff Newton, the love of her young life, to join in
with our circus. Still anticipating her first date, and undoubtedly hoping it would be with Jeff, Erica was laying all the
groundwork she could.

Jeff was getting A's in my book, as he listened attentively
and smiled at the youngsters presenting the lesson. "At least
Blair and Nolan make a good first impression," I whispered to
Brian. He scowled; the last thing he wanted was to impress *any*
boy who had an interest in Erica.

Then Chad showed up. For the first time since we'd met
him, I saw Brian smile at this event. "Chad, come on in,"
Brian called. Chad was exactly the ingredient Brian needed to
stall Erica's dating years a bit longer.

Erica cringed. Her original attraction to Chad had inverted
into a healthy dislike, and now her eyes were rolling upward in
disgust. "Just in time for refreshments," she whispered to Jeff.

"Who is that?" Jeff asked.

"My *cousin*," Erica emphasized. "By marriage."

Natalie and Gorman followed Chad with a flurry of apolo-
gies for being late. Chad grinned at Erica, who returned his ges-
ture with a tight-lipped little twitch that passed for a smile.

Ryan and Grayson disappeared into the kitchen for refreshments and soon returned with bowls of speckled pudding—a
concoction Edith had taught them—which I knew had to contain birdseed. Erica's mouth dropped open, and she looked at
me as if I were personally responsible.

"Nutritious," Ryan said.

"Delicious," Grayson said.

Go fishus, I thought. No way am I eating that stuff. They
tricked me once and I had to floss until midnight.

"Hey, Aunt Edith's pudding," Chad grunted in his monot-
one voice. He reached across Jeff for the tray Ryan was carrying, and pulled it down to peer into the bowls. Ryan let go,
thinking Chad was taking the tray from him, and the entire
tray of six bowls landed in Jeff's lap.

"Ryan!" Erica shrieked, leaping to her feet. "Chad! Look
what you're doing, you guys!"

Jeff, too, had jumped up, and was holding his shirt out to get the jiggly cold pudding away from his skin. Globs were dripping down his pants and onto his shoes.

"Oops—sorry," Ryan said.

Erica was mortified and dashed into the kitchen for some paper towels, all the while screaming, "*Do* something!" to the rest of us. The triplets took her directive to heart, and immediately began finger painting all over Jeff's legs.

Jeff backed off, trying to chuckle politely as Brian and I pulled Bennett, Cameron and Austin away from their moving easel.

"I'm terribly sorry," I said.

Just then Gizmo came up from behind Jeff and began licking his legs. Startled, Jeff jumped, shaking lumps of the pudding onto Zan's lap. Zan gasped and leaped up. Blair screamed and began to cry.

"Whoa," Chad said, bobbing his head in approval. "The guy is afraid of dogs."

"I am not afraid of dogs," Jeff said.

Erica was mopping Jeff's legs and shirt as Nick and Zan were scurrying to clean up in the kitchen. Grayson and Ryan were picking up the bowls, the triplets were rubbing pudding onto the chalkboard, and Gizmo was sniffing out hunks of the concoction that had landed on the carpet.

From down the hall you could hear Angel screeching.

"That birdseed might scratch the chalkboard," Edith warned the triplets. Delighted, they rubbed all the harder.

"Birdseed?" Jeff grimaced. "Look, I can clean all this up at home. Thanks anyway. See ya, Erica."

Erica looked ready to cry as Jeff zoomed out the driveway. She stormed off to her room.

"Ah," Brian said. "Another successful family home evening."

I hurried up to Erica's room and found her sniffling on her bed. "I'll never have any friends with such a weird family," she said. "And please don't buy me a Berenstain Bears book about this."

I bit my lip. "Okay."

"Chad is a juvenile delinquent and he scares away any

boyfriend I could ever have," Erica sobbed. "Ryan never looks what he's doing and stumbles all over everyone. Edith makes these awful desserts, and the triplets are complete maniacs. We ought to call this place Jurassic House. Dad glares at any boy who comes over, and you act like Mr. Rogers."

"Excuse me?" I said, sitting beside her on the bed.

"Just like when you conducted that museum tour for the junior high," Erica said.

"I thought that went great!" I said. The principal had asked me to take the kids to the art museum where I had worked as a guide in college. The kids with the best art grades got to go. I had thoroughly enjoyed introducing the kids to Flemish oil paintings, French tapestries and Egyptian urns. "How did that embarrass you?" I asked.

Erica sighed, pained at having to spell it out. "You were practically dancing down the halls, Mom. You were, like, *way* too enthusiastic. Just like Mr. Rogers touring a balloon factory or something."

"You know," I said, "after we got back, a *lot* of those kids thanked me and said how terrific it was."

"Oh, please," Erica said. "Those were the sixth graders, Mom. They'll kiss up to anybody."

21

OFF LIKE A HERD OF TURTLES

After eight months of employing Brian, Edith told him to take his family on a vacation. "You've earned it," she said.

"My first thought was, 'What's she going to do—install a water slide on the roof while we're gone?'" Brian admitted to me that night. "But then I realized that Edith just really wanted us to have a break."

"Well, you have been working a lot harder lately," I said. And it was true. Edith's latest invention had once again catapulted her to fame, at least in certain circles, and Brian had been twice as busy as a result.

Her new idea began with the family home evening when Jeff had gotten splattered with pudding. For weeks afterward, Erica had barely spoken to Edith, who was smart enough to trace it to the birdseed comment she had made. So to win back Erica's affection, Edith experimented with a lotion kids could rub on their skin during hot summers, to cool them off. It wouldn't just *feel* cool, it would actually lower the skin's surface temperature and maybe even prevent sunburn. Either way, Edith figured it was the kind of product that teenagers who spent lots of time in the sun would adore. "Kool Kream," she called it some days, "Heat Beater" on others. And she would put Erica's picture on the label.

Well, it backfired. Instead of cooling people off, it warmed them up. (Guess who got to be the family of guinea pigs that Edith experimented on). Just as I would have tossed out the product as a failure, Edith sold it to a mountaineering supply company, and the darned thing got taken to the top of Mount

Everest. Skiers, Arctic explorers, divers—anybody in cold climates began rubbing her "Ice Block" on their feet and hands and swearing by this new miracle cream.

When Brian told Erica how hard Edith had worked to regain her favor, she was truly touched. She even arranged for Edith to speak at a school assembly, and several kids tried her new "Ice Block" up on the auditorium stage. Edith took the occasion to announce the formation of her Scholarship for Young Inventors, an idea Brian had suggested.

"It was so cool," Erica had raved that afternoon. Obviously, tenth graders don't kiss up to just anybody.

"Well, a vacation would be wonderful," I told Brian. And maybe, I thought, it would give me more time with my daughter to convince her that I was not out to embarrass her at every opportunity. I wanted to recapture the friendship, the "girls going out to lunch" feeling that we'd had when she was younger. I would make Erica my project.

The next thing I knew, Brian and Nick had rented two motor homes and were planning a big double-family camping trip in the mountains. "Back to nature," they crowed, like two army buddies going AWOL.

As I was explaining the dates to Ryan's baseball coach, he said, "Great! Uh, I mean, this will be great for Ryan."

You mean great for the team, I thought to myself. But I couldn't blame the coach; he wanted to win, and Ryan was so far out in left field—in more ways than one—that he was sometimes a real liability.

"He's not doing so well, is he?" I asked.

The coach smiled. "Ryan probably has the highest I.Q. on the team," he said. (I must remember to tell Nick and Zan this, I thought to myself.) "But," the coach continued, "I wouldn't say he's a natural athlete."

I smiled. Poor lovable Ry.

"Don't worry about him," the coach said. "Look at Thomas Edison. I mean, people thought he was slow, but he turned out to be a genius."

I smiled. If one more person compares my kid to Thomas Edison I'm going to throttle them, I thought. Thomas Edison lived at a time when school was perfectly optional. He didn't have to worry about his S.A.T. scores, competing with computer whiz kids, or getting into the right universities. And notice that you never hear about the *mothers* of these Edison types. They probably ended up in straitjackets somewhere, I thought to myself.

"And look at Edith Horvitz!" the coach beamed. "I mean, people even thought she was crazy once!"

I stopped dead in my tracks. Now Ryan is being compared to Edith? And whaddaya mean *once?* I took a big breath. "Thank you," I said through clenched teeth. Last week Brian had had a similar experience in biting his tongue, as one of the priests complained that *his* boss was crazy.

Soon we were packing our grubbiest clothing into duffel bags and tossing them into our motor home. Nick and Zan arrived in their L. L. Beans, along with Blair and Nolan, similarly attired.

As we started up our engines, I could hear faint strains of Primary songs coming from Nick's motor home. Inside, Nolan and Blair were happily doing work pages. My own kids were already throwing potato chips and singing "The Song That Doesn't End" until you could have a head-on collision.

Three hours later, I discovered that I'd left my voice modulator at home. Edith had invented a wonderful gadget for mothers—a little portable microphone that you speak into, which drops your voice down an octave.

"I notice that kids tend to mind their dads better," Edith had said (after observing a family home evening that went completely awry when Brian had to travel to Tokyo for EE). "And I've figured out what it is."

"Men follow through better?" I guessed. "They're tougher?"

"Nope."

"They aren't around as much, so kids aren't tired of them?"

"Nope," Edith said. "It's their lower voices. I don't know why, but people pay more attention to a forceful voice. And, except for a few of us lucky gals who have stern voices naturally" (Edith blushed), "most of your deep voices belong to men."

Well, this voice theory was something I had suspected

from the outset, but it had always felt like a lame excuse when I'd thought of sharing it before. Finally, someone agreed with me!

So Edith whipped up a device to make every mother in the country sound like Bea Arthur. They were selling, too. Suddenly the kids were answering me the first time I spoke! It was a sheer miracle.

And now, here I was on a camping trip without my gadget. "Oh well," I said to Brian, "we'll have to use your voice."

"I knew there was *some* reason why I came along," Brian said.

"That," I shrugged, "and to come up with brilliant menu plans." Brian knew I was not pleased about his brainstorm to use our 72-hour emergency kit food, and see just how long we could survive on it.

Nick and Zan had agreed to do the same. The difference was that Nick and Zan's kits were four times the size of ours, and contained goodies like salmon pate and special buttery crackers they had picked up in France. Our kits contained packages of vinyl-tasting cheese that you spread onto a crumbly cracker with a little strip of red plastic for a knife.

I wasn't against emergency kits. I just believed that they were to be used for precisely that: emergencies. You expect to be inconvenienced during an emergency. That's what *makes* it an emergency. But this, I had mistakenly assumed, was a vacation.

Brian began singing "The Happy Wanderer" in his rich baritone, and soon the kids were joining in on the "ha ha ha ha ha ha" parts, laughing and falling off the furniture. I stood poised to apply ice packs (something you *never* forget when you have rowdy children), and soon I was busy wiping tears from bumped cheeks and kissing miscellaneous injuries.

Finally the wailing subsided enough for me to return to my seat up front. "That song always makes them nuts," I said, by way of blaming Brian.

He refused to take the bait, and patted my knee instead. "Camping trips always involve some scrapes and bumps," he smiled.

Erica was pouting on one of the sofas, having been opposed to this much togetherness from the beginning. When I had reminded her before the trip that we were sealed together as a family, she had looked at me with that aghast expression of hers and said, "This is supposed to be comforting news?"

I had brought along a brochure about the Indian history of the hills we were approaching, and I thought this might be the time to cheer everyone up with some folklore. "Listen up, kids," I shouted to the back of the motor home. "I want to read you something."

The kids ignored me. Erica was trying to nap, Grayson and Ryan were engrossed in comic books, and the triplets were licking their fingers and writing on the windows.

"Maybe they don't want to be read to right now," Brian suggested.

I swatted him with the brochure. The kids looked up. "Of course they do!" I said. "This is interesting!" I turned to the children. "Do you kids want me to read this to you?"

Scared to say anything else, they all chimed, "Yes! Yes!" and stopped whatever else they were doing.

"See?" I said to Brian. I then began reading about trappers, miners, Indians and regional foliage. Erica drifted off, the older two kept sneaking glances at their open comic books, and the triplets now began licking the actual windows.

"Oh, fine, then," I said. "Be uninformed."

Brian was chuckling as I threw the brochure on the floor. "When does this 72-hour starvation program begin?" I asked him.

"First thing in the morning," Brian said. "So yes, you can have the candy bar you hid in the glove compartment."

I whipped around, stunned that he'd caught me.

Brian laughed. "You are so transparent."

I snarled and ripped open my Butterfinger, then scrunched down in my seat and glanced back to make sure none of the kids could see me.

"You are also pathetic," Brian said.

"Thank you," I said. "And no, you may not have a bite. I will not share my oil with the unprepared."

"What brilliant application of a Biblical parable," Brian said, shaking his head. Then he slowly reached down into the pocket of his door and came up with a bag of peanut M&Ms.

I smiled. Great minds think alike.

Soon it was time to stop for gas, and the kids all swarmed through the mini-market. Ryan spotted fresh Churros—strips of donut-style pastries lying under a heat lamp in a pile of sugar—and alerted his conspirators that sugar and grease were within target range.

"Please? Please?" the kids all begged Brian.

"Only if you all come to the register within one minute," he said. "I am not rounding you up from all over the store."

Blair and Nolan came into the store just then, selected an apple and a pear respectively, then quietly waited beside Nick to purchase them. "Aunt Andy," Nolan said, "Did you know that right over that mountain, trappers used to sell deerskins to the miners, and then those guys would trade it to the Indians for information about gold?"

I smiled and glanced at our kids, who were arguing over whether or not there was caramel in a Mars bar.

"Right under the black walnut trees," Blair added.

"Time's up. No Churros," Brian called to our crew, taking care to roll his *R*'s.

The kids all began crying and begging. Blair and Nolan just stared at their cousins.

"You are so strict," I whispered to Brian. "They're going to remember this brittle, unbending father—"

"—and say 'that's why I'm president today,'" Brian whispered right back. "'Of course, my brothers are in an asylum because my mother was so lenient . . .'"

I pinched Brian's ribs, then herded the kids towards the door. "Come on," I said. "We have cookies and chips outside."

Just as we got to the exit, the clerk leaned around from his register, took note of my sweatshirt and said, "Oh—did you go to the Sorbonne?"

CHAPTER 22

A CLOSE ENCOUNTER
WITH ERICA

That night, in a stroke of unbelievable luck, we found a campsite with a big shower facility and a swimming pool. Within minutes the kids were doing cannonballs into the pool, yelling and splashing to their hearts' content.

Zan knocked on my door as I was getting the hamburgers ready to barbecue. "Brr," she said, dripping wet in her swimsuit. "The kids got our towels wet. Do you have any extras?"

I helped her into the motor home and gave her a dry towel. "We're thinking of sleeping in a tent tonight," she said.

"You don't want to stay in your motor home?" I asked.

"Oh, no," she said, tycoon-turned-camper. "Nolan and Blair want to sleep under the stars and look for constellations." But of course.

Nick popped in just then with his children. "Did you see a fast, skinny woman come through here?" he asked.

I laughed and nodded to the back of the motor home where Zan was still shivering.

"Dry off," Nick said, helping her pat her legs. "You're cold because your surface to mass ratio is too high. The amount of skin surface you have, compared to the amount of fat and muscle bulk, is greater than average. That's why you get so cold." Then Nick turned to me. "Hey, Andy—" he called.

"I don't want to know about my surface to mass ratio," I said.

Nick chuckled. "I was just going to ask if you'd like to sleep outside and rough it with us tonight." I smiled and Nick knew my answer. "Face it, Andy. You're a wuss."

"That's Mrs. Wuss to you," I said. "Mosquitoes eat 87 times their weight every hour, and I see no reason to become part of their food chain."

"You are making that up," Nick said. Nick is probably the only guy in the state who actually knows the dietary habits of mosquitoes—plus countless other trivia—and therefore catches me every time I invent a statistic to serve my purposes. "Well, try to keep the TV down," he winked, and they headed back to the pool.

After the food was ready, I went to the pool to ask Brian when he thought the kids would be ready to eat. I caught him shouting, "If you don't get out of the pool when I say one hour is up, then I'll make you get out in *half* an hour!"

"Amazing," I whispered. "And you majored in math."

Brian jumped, then blushed at the illogical threat he had just shouted for all to hear.

"Let's see," I continued, "thirty minutes minus sixty minutes . . ."

"Oh hush," he said.

"Uncle Brian," Nolan called from the shallow end. "That didn't make sense."

"Trust that kid to catch me," Brian muttered. Then he shouted, "It was just a joke, Nolan."

"This is better than when Grayson ran for treasurer in the sixth grade," I said to Brian. Grayson had filled out the application form with "tresherer" as his desired position. (And he won—obviously spelling was not a prerequisite.)

"Okay, okay," Brian said, pulling me onto his chaise lounge and tickling me.

Erica saw us from a chair on the other side of the pool, and quickly glanced around the campsite for other teenagers who might notice her parents creating a scene.

"Hey," I whispered to Brian. "If you guys don't want to eat yet, maybe I'll go for a walk with Erica." Brian nodded and I headed over to her. "Having a good time?" I called out.

Erica gave me one of her "no—duh" glances.

"Would you like to go for a walk?" I asked.

Erica looked at the younger kids splashing and screaming,

then shrugged and got up. "Anything's better than this," she said.

We walked down the road to a footpath, then headed down a bushy hill.

"Do you ever make wishes?" I asked.

Erica shrugged. "Not really."

"Boy, I do," I said.

Erica smirked and nodded as if to say, "that figures."

I took a deep breath and tried again. "I mean, you think about the future, right?"

"Doesn't everyone?"

"Sure," I said. "Sometimes I think about what it will be like when you're all grown up. I wonder about your career, the kind of man you'll marry, what your kids will be like. Do you ever think of those things?"

"I guess so." Erica pulled a leaf off a bush as she passed by, and stepped over a tree root.

"I used to wonder what kind of man I'd marry," I said. The path turned left and stopped at the edge of a ravine. "Hey, look at that—a river!"

Erica turned to go back. "You want to tell the others?"

I watched it rising and falling along its path and listened to the spray as it tumbled over boulders and fallen trees. "Not yet," I said. "Let's just the two of us enjoy it for awhile."

Erica and I stepped sideways down the slope, pushing showers of pebbles onto the banks below. At the river's edge we pulled off our shoes and waded in up to our ankles. "Pretty cold," I said. Erica nodded.

"So did you picture Dad?" she asked.

"Huh?"

"You were saying you used to imagine who you'd marry."

"Oh," I said. "Actually, no. I thought I'd marry someone with dark hair and flashing eyes. I pictured him with one of those jawlines you see in sketches of menswear in the newspaper."

Now Erica laughed. "That's not Dad."

I thought of my blonde, balding eternal sweetheart and smiled. "Nope," I said. "I did a lot better. Your father is the greatest companion a girl could have. Even better than my dreams."

Erica was rolling her eyes.

"He really is," I said, splashing her for not believing me.

Erica splashed me back, then stepped lightly onto a fallen tree and sat down, dangling her feet in the water. I chose a rock a few feet out in the river, and sat down facing her as the water rushed around me.

"Sometimes I wonder what *our* relationship will be like," I said.

Erica gave me a grand sigh then, as though I had taken her on this excursion just so we could have an uncomfortable little chat.

"Please don't shut me out, Erica," I said. "I want us to love each other. When you're all grown up and married, I want us to be friends. Sometimes you seem so distant—it scares me. I don't know what I'd do if I lost you."

"Oh, Mom." Erica kicked her foot in the water.

"I know I must do things that embarrass you sometimes—"

"Most times," Erica said with a grimace.

"You know," I said, "you've embarrassed me once or twice, yourself."

Erica was stunned. "When?"

"Well, let's see," I said, leaning back on my rock and trying to choose from the vast array of examples. "One time your father tried to give me singing lessons. You were about five years old at the time. Dad was showing me how to tighten my diaphragm under my rib cage, when the phone rang. You picked it up and told a woman from the ward that I was busy with my diaphragm and couldn't come to the phone."

Erica just stared at me until it sunk in. Then she smiled. "I did that?"

"Yes ma'am, you did," I said. "Naturally your father thought it was brilliant, and only wished he'd thought of it himself."

Erica chuckled, and twirled a twig between her fingers. "But I was just a little kid."

"True," I admitted. "But I don't have too many stories about you as a grown-up." I watched her, my baby girl who had somehow become a young woman overnight. "I hope I *will* have some of those," I said.

Erica looked up, puzzled.

"Stories about you as a grown-up," I said. "I know you get mad at me sometimes and you think I'm 'uncool,' but I love you so much, Erica. I picture being a grandma to your children someday. I imagine us sharing holidays and memories—vacations, even." Erica watched the swift current below her feet. "It's hard to be a mother," I went on. "It's a wonderful job, but it's also the toughest one. I know I've made a lot of mistakes, but I hope you'll realize that I'm just human and—"

"Mom, *please.*" Erica was reaching lecture overload.

I paused, letting silence fill in the space where I wanted to tell her again and again that I loved her and wanted to be her friend. "Well, I guess we should be getting back," I said, brushing off my legs and scooting off my boulder.

Suddenly my shoe caught on a piece of fishing line that was stuck in a crevice of the boulder. I lost my footing and tumbled into the river head first. Icy water swirled around me, pushing me against the stone. With my shoe still entangled in the line, I couldn't pull my feet down under me to stand or climb out. Arching my back, I came up for air and saw Erica splashing through the river towards me.

"Mom!" she was screaming. "Mom!"

I tried to flip over so I could reach up and free my foot, but the current was too strong. As I bobbed up again, gasping for breath, I saw Erica's hand reaching for me. I thrust one arm up out of the water just as the line snapped, and the river jerked me down under and away from Erica's reach. My skin was aching with the cold, and all I could hear was the roar of the tumbling rocks and water.

Somehow I kicked my way to the surface again and gulped more air. I grabbed at branches and rocks as the river carried me downstream. Looking back for Erica, I saw her trying to wade towards me. "Go back!" I yelled.

I tried to swim toward the bank, but the river seemed stronger than ever. I looked for a bush or a rock—anything to grab and hold onto. Finally I saw a tree that had fallen

halfway into the river, and I prayed fervently that I could get
to it.

Suddenly the river pulled me under again, then surged
out of a hole and slammed me into the fallen tree. I threw
my arms over it and clung to the bark, praying my gratitude.
I looked back for Erica, but couldn't see her.

"Mom!" I looked to my right, and there was Erica running
along the bank. Crying hysterically, she climbed out onto the
tree and reached down to help me up. Fighting against the current and scraping my stomach against the tree, I held Erica's
hand and pulled myself onto the top. We stumbled onto the
bank and collapsed, holding each other and crying.

"I love you, Mom," Erica sobbed.

I held her and said a silent prayer of thanks. For a few
minutes neither of us spoke as I tried to catch my breath. I
smoothed her hair and looked into her precious face. "Thank
you for saving me."

"Oh, Mom," Erica cried. "I thought you were going to drown.
I was so scared."

"Me too," I said, shivering. Erica started pulling off her T-
shirt to wrap around me, but I held up a hand to stop her. "I'll
be okay," I said. "I shouldn't have climbed out onto that rock.
I didn't realize how deep the water was."

Erica hugged me, rubbing my aching arms to warm me
up. "Please forgive me for treating you the way I have," she
said. "I've been terrible."

I kissed her forehead and cried. "I love you," I whispered.
"I hope you'll forgive me, too."

We hugged again and Erica wiped her tears. "You didn't
realize how deep the water was," she said, "and I didn't realize how deep my love was. I really am glad you're my mom."

I smiled and we pulled each other to our feet.

"Can you walk?" Erica asked.

My legs were sore and stiff with cold, but I nodded. We
headed back to the camp arm in arm, grateful to be alive,
grateful for each other.

Brian looked up as he saw us coming, and took off his sunglasses. He smiled as I got closer. "New hairdo, Andy?"

"Oh, Dad," Erica said, throwing her arms around him. "Mom nearly drowned!"

Brian glanced at his soaking wet wife and said, "This I gotta hear." But as Erica unfolded the story, Brian leaped up in alarm, wrapped me in towels and called the kids out of the pool. Nick and Zan rushed over, too. Wanting to see where it all happened, they herded the children to the ridge of the ravine, but forbade them to go any farther.

"I'm not letting you out of my sight," Brian said, keeping a protective arm around me and rubbing my cold arms. "Let's get you into bed."

"I'm fine now," I said. "Erica loves me."

"You mean Erica saved you," Grayson corrected me.

"She did," I said. "But this is much more important."

CHAPTER 23

THE HISTORY LESSON

Despite its disastrous start, the rest of the trip went smoothly. Well, as smoothly as a trip can go which has a three-day moratorium on edible food. Our 72-hour kits were only one notch better than starvation, leaving our stomachs rumbling and our children grumbling. When we finally returned to regular food I thought the kids would cry tears of joy.

As we drove into Edith's driveway a week later, Brian slammed on the brakes. There, all over the sprawling lawn, were dozens of huge wooden cows.

"Hey," Ryan pointed out with delight, "It looks like a *Far Side* cartoon!"

"It certainly does," Brian sang through his teeth. Then he whispered to me, "I *knew* she'd pull something while we were gone. What do you want to bet they glow in the dark?"

I stared at the plywood Holsteins. One day the place was French Victorian, then whammo! Country.

"One week!" Brian went on. "We were only gone one week!" He drove on slowly, as if we were creeping through a sacred burial ground.

"I like them," Cameron said.

"Look at that one." Austin and Bennett were giggling, and pointing to a cow in the middle. "It has on a hat."

Sure enough, Edith had crocheted saucy little berets for three of the herd. No doubt more were in the works.

"Shanell's mom has two wooden cows in front and some sheep in back," Erica said. "And they're really cute. But this is, like, a population explosion."

"Maybe someone will thin their herd," Brian suggested. "You know, for the sake of the species."

"Brian," I said. "You are not taking down Edith's cows in the middle of the night."

Brian pretended to be stunned that I would accuse him of such a thing. *"Moi?"*

I gave him the same glance I give the kids when they're crossing the line and they know it.

"I didn't say me," Brian continued. "I said someone. Besides, taking them down wasn't even on my mind."

"No," I said, "blowing them to smithereens was."

"Right," Brian said. "Why can't she do anything in moderation? Isn't this much red meat against the Word of Wisdom?"

"Well, just be glad the yard isn't full of *live* animals," I said. "Besides, we have to remember, it's her house."

Brian sighed. "I just keep telling myself that soon we'll get a teaching offer and—zzzooom!" Brian sliced his hand through the air like an airplane. Just before our trip, our realtor had said he might be getting an offer on our old house. That would certainly help us buy a new home wherever Brian got hired.

"Welcome home!" Edith called, waving from the porch. "You missed homemaking night. Guess what we made!"

"Gee," Brian said, rubbing his chin and pretending to guess. "Cows?"

"Yup," Edith said, rocking proudly on her heels. "I made the most of anyone."

"Well, who says quality is more important than quantity?" Brian said. "Good for you, Edith."

The kids all ran to hug Edith hello, then began telling the stories of our campout. They started with my near-drowning, gave a critical review of our 72-hour emergency food, and finished with a blow-by-blow account of a skunk that crept into Uncle Nick's tent one night and scared Aunt Zan half to death.

"I'm so glad you're alive," Edith said, hugging me with tears in her eyes. I hugged her back, and thought about how much I was going to miss her when we moved. Cows and all.

That night we decided to pack our camping gear together in a storage closet upstairs, to save rummaging all over the next time we went camping ("Next time?" I asked. I stared at my family the same way a woman does who has just delivered a baby, and someone asks about her *next* child).

Brian laughed and pushed me up the stairs. I couldn't help thinking, as I lugged the gear up to the third floor, that maybe everyone would forget where it was.

"How about in here?" Austin shouted, swinging open a door to a room filled with boxes of Christmas decorations.

"No, here—" Grayson said, dropping a sleeping bag at the doorway to a bedroom full of furniture that must have belonged to Edith's aunt.

"Not enough room," Brian said, peering into both of these choices.

"Mom, look!" Erica was calling from a room at the far end of the hall. As the boys found an empty bedroom and began loading their stuff into it, I went to see what Erica had discovered.

"This room was locked before," she said, speaking in hushed tones and stepping carefully into a girl's bedroom. "I remember trying the doorknob, because it's the only porcelain one."

I followed her into the musty room where a once-white lace bedspread covered the faded pink bedding of a small girl. Antique dolls were carefully arranged on the bed and in a wicker buggy with metal wheels. They wore intricate dresses, fur muffs and tiny leather boots that laced.

Frayed lace curtains hung in dust-laden scallops at the windows, and an old vanity of inlaid wood, with a round mirror, stood against one wall. Books with cracked bindings rested in a small bookcase; above it hung an old movie poster in a wooden frame, depicting a little girl in a flapper costume, posing with a sultry woman in a fur-collared coat and a dapper gentleman with his hair parted down the middle.

"Oh my," I whispered, not daring to touch anything for fear it would crumble in my fingers.

"Look at this," Erica said, creaking open a closet door.

There hung dozens of little dresses, and tiny satin shoes in every color imaginable. Hat boxes were stacked on a shelf, and under one was a thick black scrapbook.

"I wonder if Edith knows about this room," I said. "I'll bet it belonged to one of her cousins."

"She must have really been a movie fan," Erica said, pulling a stack of playbills from the bookcase. "I'll bet this stuff's worth a lot to collectors."

"Be careful," I said. "Maybe Edith wants to sell them."

"You think she knows about this room?"

"Well, if it was locked before and now it's open . . ." I shrugged.

Erica replaced the playbills and reached up for the scrapbook.

"I feel like we're snooping," I said, glancing nervously toward the door.

Erica flashed me a broad grin. "Yeah!" she enthused.

I wanted to tell her to leave the scrapbook alone, but I was dying to see it myself. Carefully I helped her rest it on the bed, and we crouched over it, turning the brittle pages.

"Oh," Erica sighed, disappointed. "I thought it would be some of Edith's family pictures, but it's just more old movie stuff. No wonder Edith left it here."

"Look," I said. "Here's a smaller version of that same poster." I pointed to the book, then to the flapper girl on the wall. Suddenly I caught my breath, blinking in shock until Erica had to grab my arm and almost shake me.

"What's the matter?" she said.

"That's Baby Edie," I whispered, pointing to the wall. "Do you remember her? She was a huge childhood star, just before Shirley Temple."

Erica shrugged, and now I grabbed *her* arm. "Erica," I said. "That's Edith Horvitz!"

Erica stared at the poster and shook her head. "Are you sure?"

"It has to be," I said, now flipping through the scrapbook for more photos of Edith. "Look!"

Near the back of the book was a newspaper clipping about

Baby Edie's parents dying in a plane crash. According to the article, Baby Edie, about nine at the time, was so distraught that she was hospitalized, and would now be raised by an aunt.

"She never made another movie," I whispered. "I remember reading about her years ago. She just . . . vanished."

"I never heard of her," Erica said.

"Brian!" I called, stepping into the hallway just as the guys were heading downstairs.

"Oh, there you are," he said. "I wondered what happened to you two."

"Come and see this!" I shouted. "Edith was Baby Edie!"

"What!" Brian came into the room and his jaw dropped. When I showed him the article and the movie poster, he just whistled and shook his head. "Amazing," he whispered.

We all just stared silently as I turned the pages of the scrapbook and we saw pictures of the old plays and films Edith had starred in. Even then, Edith's character was mischievous. One poster depicted her as a slingshot-toting little firebrand on a cruise ship. Another showed her in a coonskin hat, pouting, with her arms crossed over a shotgun.

"I thought Baby Edie was just a child star who gave up show biz," he said. "Few of them last, and . . . I guess everyone forgot about her when Shirley Temple came along . . ."

Erica turned to him with her hands on her hips. "So . . . some historian," she teased her father.

"It makes such sense," Brian said. "I'll bet this house was actually Edith's, and when her aunt got custody, she took over the mansion for herself."

"And with Edith in the hospital, so distraught over the deaths of her parents . . ." I said, feeling real sorrow for the little girl Edith used to be.

Erica shrugged. "That's what made Edith crazy."

"Who said Edith was crazy?" Brian and I said in unison. We had so carefully avoided labeling her in front of the children.

Erica smiled. "Like it isn't obvious?"

I smiled. "But now we know why! Poor Edith. Couldn't you just cry for that little girl?"

"So sad . . ." Brian said, glancing around the room.

"Shall we tell her we found out?" I asked.

Brian thought for a minute. "I'm not sure Edith remembers any of this," he said. "I'm serious. She's never said a word about it." He had a point. Edith once mentioned that she couldn't remember her childhood and had blamed it on shock therapy.

Just then we heard Edith's voice calling from the other end of the hall. "Hey," she bellowed. "You've got three kids asking for Velcro jackets down here." This was her version of a warning that the kids were running wild. We heard her steps getting closer.

"Oh my gosh," I whispered. "Quick! Hide the scrapbook."

Erica dashed to the closet with it as Brian went out to run interference.

"Oh—you found my old bedroom," Edith said before Brian could speak. "You'll never believe what's in there." Edith casually led the way right back into her room, where Erica and I both gulped.

"Can you believe all this?" Edith said, waving her hand to include the entire room. "This was mine. 'Course I never got to spend much time here, on account of my aunt. She shipped me from one hospital to another, and put this house in her own name."

I glanced at Brian, who blushed at being right.

"If I wasn't crazy by the time I went in," Edith said, "I guarantee you I was by the time I came out."

"Oh, Edith," I said, throwing my arms around her. "We had no idea you'd been through such a terrible ordeal."

Edith shrugged. "Me neither! But I turned out okay," she said.

Erica's eyes bulged, but she kept quiet.

"I found this room while you guys were on your vacation," Edith said. "The minute I walked in, it hit me. I remembered almost everything. Look at this." Edith lifted a doll from its tiny carriage. "A Baby Edie doll. That was me. Baby Edie. She looks just like me, huh?"

We smiled at the replica of Edith's movie posters, then at

the aging woman holding the past in her hands. "She's beautiful," I whispered.

"No wonder I always thought I'd be famous," Edith said. "It's because I was!" Edith cackled with delight. "I used to think I had dreamed about being an actress. What it really was, was actual memories."

"Your aunt was so mean," Erica said.

"Erica," I whispered and shook my head.

"Meaner than a mule chewing on a bee," Edith agreed. "And that's a fact." Brian and I chuckled as Edith continued. "You talk about greedy and matriculating."

"You mean manipulating?" Brian asked.

"That's right," Edith said.

"It must have been a terrible blow to lose your parents," I said, almost afraid to bring it up but not wanting to miss the chance to express sympathy.

"I guess so," Edith said. "I don't remember much about them. I really spent my whole childhood making movies. I'm sure I was upset, as any kid would be. But my aunt exaggerated it to the press so she could get my house and my money."

"Such a tough way to grow up," I said.

Edith smiled. "You kidding? I'm lucky as a horseshoe."

Just then we heard a crash and ran out into the hall.

"Nobody's bleeding," Ryan called up the stairs. This had become our standard concern whenever there was a crash.

"Tell you what I'll do," Edith said as we all hurried down the stairs. "I'll plan a special family home evening this Monday, and we can even watch a Baby Edie movie. I been wanting to see one, myself."

We all exchanged excited glances, then went to clean up the tower of Bennett's blocks that Gizmo had knocked over with his tail.

CHAPTER 24

THE SECRET SHARED

The next morning, our realtor called with just the news we'd been waiting for. A family had offered the full asking price on our house, and they were even prequalified. Brian and I couldn't wait to sign the papers.

By Monday we had the biggest turnout ever for our family home evening. Not only did everybody want to congratulate us on selling our house, but they couldn't wait to hear about Edith's secret past.

Even Jeff Newton decided to take his chances with Brian's glares and Edith's birdseed pudding, to be with Erica. Natalie brought Chad, who—amazingly—was dressed like a normal person. "I gave him an ultimatum," Natalie mentioned casually in the kitchen to me. "I said either clean up your act or I'll embarrass you in front of your friends."

I was surprised and delighted at her new strength. Instead of shrinking and feeling sorry for herself, Natalie was really taking responsibility and getting tough with that kid.

Natalie chuckled. "I told him I'd ask you for all your secrets about how you embarrass *your* kids, and he went out and got a haircut that very afternoon."

I forced a smile. "So glad I could help."

But most amazing of all was when my mother showed up with Vivian Halpert, the neighbor she had despised for so many years. "What gives?" I whispered to her as Grayson took Mrs. Halpert on a quick tour.

"Well, I accidentally hit their garbage cans," Mom said.

"And this mended your relationship?"

"Let me finish," Mom snapped. "So it went rolling down the street, and naturally I had to chase it and carry it back. I was just about to put it on the curb when Vivian came out of her house. She took one look at me"—Mom lowered her voice now, and took my arm—"and burst into *tears*. Can you believe that? She thought I was carrying her cans in for her, doing a good deed."

I smiled. A friendship built by accident.

"Well, it meant so much to her," Mom said, "that I couldn't just say, 'I hit your can and I was bringing it back,' so I carried them all in. What else could I do?"

I laughed, picturing my mother hefting someone else's garbage cans for them.

"Next thing I know, Vivian brings me a cake. German chocolate." Mom nodded to remind me that this happens to be her favorite. "And I think to myself, maybe these people aren't so bad. Maybe doing some nice things for them won't kill me."

"Maybe you'll even rack up a lemon pie or two," I said.

"Don't be smart." Mom glanced around to make sure Mrs. Halpert couldn't hear her. "So I thought I'd invite her to family home evening. Who knows."

I smiled. "I am really glad to hear this," I said. "Honest."

Mom shrugged, as though she forgave old enemies all the time, and turned to go out and join the others.

"Hey, Mom," I said. "Are you limping?"

Mom turned around. "Oh, didn't I tell you about that? I dropped one of Vivian's trash cans on my foot and bruised it."

"You're kidding. Are you sure nothing's broken?"

Mom smirked. "Andy," she said, as I suddenly saw where Erica's strained impatience came from, "Gorman is a *foot* doctor. He saw me that very night. A house call." Now she raised her eyebrows again to indicate that I should be impressed. "He's such a fine young man. Said I'll be fine."

I smiled. "Well, good then."

Mom shrugged. "This too shall pass."

Soon everyone had gathered in the living room, and Edith brought out her scrapbook. "Most of you know that I was orphaned as a little girl and raised by my aunt," she said. "I spent a lot of time in the hospital, and then I won the Nobel prize."

Everyone laughed at this incredible condensation.

"Now I'm gonna fill in some blanks," Edith said, joining in the laughter. She opened the black scrapbook and said, "This was me as a little girl."

"But that's Baby Edie," Mrs. Halpert exclaimed. "I was a big fan of hers."

Edith smiled. "Well, you're lookin' at her."

Mrs. Halpert gasped. Admittedly, Edith is a shock to those who've never seen her before, with her thinning hair and nearly black lipstick. "See, kids?" Edith said. "This is what show biz does to people." Then she threw her head back and cackled.

The kids were all buzzing with confusion now; they'd never heard of Baby Edie. So Edith quieted them down and explained her old movie career, even letting them handle her Baby Edie doll.

Nick and Zan beamed. "She still has the old charisma," Nick smiled. Paula, Natalie, and my mother were in shock.

Edith then explained, not mincing any words, about her aunt, Fanny Drossett, and how Edith had virtually forgotten that she'd ever been an actress. The kids huddled together at Edith's feet, enthralled with the tale of a real-life villain.

"But let me tell you how lucky I really am," Edith said. "When I was about eleven, I got to meet Dr. Frederick DuMonde, who was then a famous doctor. He was actually a chemist. We took to each other right away. In fact, when I think of a dad, Dr. DuMonde is the man who comes to my mind. He's the one who got me interested in chemistry. He used to bring all his chemistry books to me in the hospital and we'd talk for hours about the things I'd been reading."

Brian smiled at me. Edith was born to captivate an audience.

"My other interest was crocheting, because that's what they had us do in the hospital. If I wasn't studying chemistry, I was making sweaters and blankets for all the other patients. I still love it today. I guess you've noticed."

Everyone chuckled.

"So you see?" Edith said. "If I had stayed in the movie business, I would never have become an inventor. We wouldn't have Stick 'Em Up Glue, and I would never have won the Nobel prize."

I looked around at the faces of my family. They were beaming, every one.

"But even better than that," Edith said, "was getting active in the Church again. My folks had converted and had me baptized, but I never knew a thing about it until Andy Taylor came to my door and got me to be the homemaking leader."

I smiled with tears in my eyes. I had been so wrong about Edith, so quick to misjudge her.

"My testimony means more to me than any movie career, hit record or Nobel prize ever could," Edith said. "And you folks who know me, know that one thing Edith Horvitz cannot do, is lie."

The children were nodding, taking in every word.

"The Taylors have been a better family to me than any I could ever have hoped for," Edith said. "And that makes me the luckiest woman in the world." Edith smiled at me and I couldn't stop the tears from running down my cheeks.

"Well, enough blubbering," Edith said, slapping a videotape into her machine. "Time to watch me on TV."

Brian and I chuckled, and I noticed that even his eyes were moist. Could it be that Brian Taylor had finally found a soft spot in his heart for Edith Horvitz?

The movie began with a little girl riding toward the camera on a pony. Thick ringlets bounced as she trotted closer. Just as she got close enough for her smiling face to fill the screen, old-fashioned lettering read, *The Littlest Mountie* starring Baby Edie."

"Hoo—eee!" Edith bellowed. "Look at all that hair!"

CHAPTER 25

LIFE WITH A TWIST

That Wednesday Brian got a call from a university in Ohio, wanting him to fly out for an interview. "Andy!" he screamed, dashing into the kitchen and whirling me around. "Pack your bags, honey! We did it!"

"Oh, Brian!" I exulted. "This is wonderful!"

He showed me a map of the city where we'd be moving, and then its proximity to all of the exciting cities back east. The salary was perfect, and we'd finally have a house of our own. "Let's wait until after the interview to tell the kids," Brian said. "Just in case."

Edith, of course, knew this was what Brian had been waiting for, and slapped him on the back. "Congratulations," she said. "You folks deserve the very best."

Brian caught an early flight the next morning, and by Saturday afternoon he was home with a firm job offer. "They want me to start in two weeks! I want to take the whole family out to dinner to celebrate," he said. "Andy, I saw the prettiest homes. You will love it there—and they have the four seasons."

"Wonderful! I exclaimed. "I *love* that hotel. It must be a pretty cosmopolitan—"

"Andy," Brian said, shaking his head, "you are so L.A."

I stared at him, and then it hit me. "Wait—you're talking about the actual *seasons*, aren't you?" I blushed.

I could hardly contain my excitement as we announced the joyous news to the children. "Just think—we'll have white Christmases," I said. The kids smiled. Oh, well, I thought. You can't expect children to get excited about something they've never experienced.

I went into the triplets' room and found Austin with tears in his eyes, clutching a crocheted bunny. "Does this mean we'll be leaving Ant Eater?" Austin asked.

"Oh, honey," I said, kneeling down to hug him. "We can come back for a visit. And maybe Aunt Edith will come out and see us. We can invite her for Christmas. Wouldn't that be fun?"

Austin sniffled. "But I like it here."

"You'll like it there, too," I said. "Honest."

I stepped into the hall where Brian was carrying boxes to our bedroom. "No more wooden cows!" he whispered, his eyes dancing. "No more glowing house! No more crocheted office chairs!"

I followed him to the bedroom where he began packing some of his books. "And Erica should be thrilled," he continued. "No more Chad to drive her crazy." He glanced at me, wiggling his eyebrows. "No more scrambled home evenings, either, with everybody and their dog showing up. How many people were here last week— fifty?"

I smiled at his exaggeration. "Thirty or so," I said.

Brian whistled. "Free at last," he almost shouted.

I went down the hall to Ryan's room. He was slowly loading a box with knick-knacks (his room was finally looking pretty good) as I walked in.

"Oh, hi," he said.

"What's the matter?" I asked.

Ryan shrugged. "Nothing."

"You seem sad or something. Don't you want to move?"

"Sure," he said, a sudden lilt in his voice. "I mean, this is what we've wanted."

"Yeah," I said, purposely injecting enthusiasm into my voice.

I checked on Grayson. He was slouched down on his bed reading a paperback, as if the big news hadn't registered. "Don't you want to pack, or call your friends, or—or dance down the hall or something?" I asked him.

"I will," he said, flipping a page.

I couldn't understand it. The kids should be elated. But instead, they were acting as indifferent as the unflappable Archers, Zan's parents.

"Great news, huh?" I said as I popped my head into Erica's room.

Erica was staring out the window at the front lawn, and turned suddenly when I walked in. "Oh, hi. Yeah, it's just— all of a sudden, I guess. I need a minute to get used to the idea."

"Oh, of course you do," I said, sitting on her bed. "Moving is a big event, especially to another state. I think we'll all need a period of adjustment. Are you worried about leaving your friends? Jeff?"

Erica came and sat beside me. "No, that isn't it. I mean, I'll miss them, but...I don't know what it is." She smiled and leaned against my shoulder. "I'll be fine."

I patted her leg. "A new adventure," I said.

Erica smiled. "Yeah."

Brian had thought of even more reasons to feel giddy when I got back to our bedroom. "We will no longer have to endure comparisons between our kids and Nick's," he said. "They can excel their hearts out, and we'll be miles away!" Brian was labeling boxes with a big black marker. "MSTR BDRM," he wrote.

"I love my Mom," I said, with a huge "but" at the end of the sentence.

Brian hugged me. "I know," he said. "But now if she wants to criticize you, she'll have to call long distance."

"And Natalie will have to rely on her own wits to raise Chad," I said, thinking of the countless times she had called me for advice.

"Paula will have to find a new sounding board, too," Brian said, reminding me of the hours I'd spent supplementing Paula's therapist. "Good grief," Brian laughed. "What will you do with all your free time?"

We hugged and kept packing. "It's been hard for you, working for Edith," I said.

Brian gave me a "you have no idea," glance.

"Remember the time she stuck the triplets on that Velcro wall?" I said.

Brian laughed. "Trust Edith. And of course I'll never forget her glue," he said, patting the top of his head where she had glued the toupee in England.

"How about the time she fired those movie producers who wanted to make a story of her life?" I said.

"She is really something," Brian agreed.

"Scented earrings, dog mints, mood paint—" I shook my head.

"There's only one Edith," Brian said.

Just then there was a knock on our door. "Sister Horvitz is out on the front lawn pulling up her cows," Erica said.

Brian and I dashed downstairs and out the front door.

"Edith," I called, "what are you doing?"

Edith placed a wooden cow on a stack of four others, and turned. Her eyes were red from crying and she brushed a tear from one cheek. "Thought I'd give you folks a goin' away present," she said. "These are the cows I named after you."

Brian and I could only sputter in amazement.

"This one is Erica," she said. "See the long lashes? I painted ballet slippers on her, too."

I smiled, shaking my head in disbelief.

"And here's Brian," she went on, pulling the next one off the pile. "Notice I made him bald under the beret." She waved at Brian. "You told me you like bein' bald, so fine with me."

"These three little calves are the triplets," Edith said. "Look at the mischief in this one's eyes—now that's Austin to a tee."

Brian and I couldn't help laughing at Edith's personalized livestock. All this time they'd been on the front lawn and we'd had no idea we were so lavishly immortalized.

Edith then pointed out the spots on Ryan's cow that were shaped like the jigsaw puzzle pieces he so adored. Grayson's cow was mooing, to depict the fact that Grayson had inherited Brian's wonderful singing voice.

Finally she came to mine. "Now this one's blushing," Edith said. "It's anybody's guess what she's done this time!"

"Oh, Edith," I laughed. "These are incredible. You are truly amazing."

"We'll cherish them," Brian said.

Edith's lip quivered again, and she turned away, unable to speak.

I stepped out to hug Edith, and Brian joined us. "Andy," he said, "I've gotta talk to you."

I looked up at my husband and saw tears in his eyes. We stepped into the foyer and Brian took a deep breath. "I know you and the kids are really excited about this move," he said. "We've been praying to get a new job, I've promised you a new house—Andy, I love you with all my heart, and I just don't know how to tell you this, but—

"But you want to stay?" I asked, eager to supply the words. "You think maybe this move is a mistake?" I said. For the first time in a week, I felt a genuinely warm feeling in my chest.

Brian led me into the living room and we sat on one of Edith's crocheted sofas. Brian bent over and held his head in his hands. When he sat up, he was crying. "I want to stay. I mean, if that's all right with you and the kids," he said. "I feel that all this time we've been praying for a job, and the answer was right here under our noses."

"We're staying?" a voice squeaked from the hallway. It was Erica, grinning from ear to ear.

"I think so," I said, smiling and crying all at once.

"Hey, you guys!" Erica shouted, bounding up the stairs two at a time.

"But what about working for Edith?" I whispered to Brian.

"I..." Brian shrugged and then laughed, wiping tears he couldn't explain from his shining eyes. "She needs me, don't you think?"

I wrapped my arms around Brian's middle as we leaned back on the sofa. "I think you need Edith," I said.

"What?"

"I think we all need Edith," I said. "And Nick and Zan and Mom and Natalie—all of them." Brian looked at me, puzzled.

"It's like the Church," I said, sitting up. "It throws you together with all these people you might never choose to work with, but there you are. You're forced to compromise and get along and...the next thing you know, you've developed qualities that..."

Brian smiled. "That's it," he said. "The refiner's fire. The way we're polished by adversity. I guess you can't run from every challenge and take the easy way out."

"We could," I said. "But we probably wouldn't grow."

Brian closed his eyes. "I'm going to have to put up with all these relatives?" He winced.

I laughed. "All of them. Hey, we're sealed!"

Brian's eyes zinged open in the stark realization that if all went well, Natalie would make it to the temple and Chad would become an eternal fixture on our family tree. "Great Scott!" he gasped.

"If we can't get along with them here," I mused, "how can we hope to get along with them in the next life?"

Brian just stared at the ceiling. "You're right," he said. "This is what life's about, isn't it? Not running away, but— working through." Somehow, Brian and I had discovered the joy at the center of sacrifice. You think you're miserable until you give all you can—and suddenly you see that you weren't diminishing, but expanding. That's when the gratitude and joy emerge.

We could hear all the children cheering and celebrating upstairs now, running and stomping to their hearts' content.

I hugged him again. "What about teaching? Won't you miss it?"

Brian smiled. "I can teach at church. It's all right. It really is. Edith is, well, Edith. But...I think I've grown accustomed to her. I sound like Henry Higgins, don't I?"

"You sound like someone who's figured out the purpose of life," I said. "Not many folks do that, y'know."

Brian smiled. "So we live with the wooden cows and the-birdseed pudding..."

"I can't imagine how we were ever happy without them," I laughed. "Let's tell Edith."

By now the kids had thundered down the stairs and the whole Taylor clan burst out onto the lawn like a flock of startled pigeons. "Edith!" I shouted. "We're not moving!"

Edith turned, her face a priceless picture of absolute shockand delight. "You mean it?" she said.

"That is, if I still have a job," Brian said.

Edith threw her arms around Brian, nearly knocking him down. "Hot dog! I never prayed for anything so hard in my life!"

"So you were the one," Brian said, wagging a finger at her.

Edith whirled him around, dancing him around the wooden cow-strewn lawn like Julie Andrews in a "Sound of Music" out-take.

"What changed your mind?" Edith asked, stopping suddenly.

Brian shrugged, then pointed to his chest. "Something in here," he said. "I just felt we should stay."

Edith beamed, then hugged the kids. "You happy?" she asked them.

They all spoke at once, excitedly assuring her how thrilled they were.

Now Edith gave me a hug. "We make a good team," she said to me.

I laughed and hugged her back. "I think you're right," I said. And I have to admit, I really meant it.

Just then a dusty brown trailer van pulled into the driveway, blaring Latin music and swaying on its tires as if it might tip over.

"Oh," Edith said, jogging down the driveway. "That must be the Candelarios."

"You mean candelabras?" I asked.

"No," Edith said, "My Argentines."

"Your what?" Brian said.

"The Flying Candelarios," Edith said. Then, waving at the dark, smiling faces inside the truck, she bellowed, "Aloha!"

"Doesn't she mean hola?" Ryan whispered.

"What Argentines?" Brian persisted.

"The folks who are gonna train the macaws," Edith called back, directing the van to the side of the house.

"What macaws?" I shouted. Angel was more than enough macaw for one lifetime.

Edith glanced back at the road just as a smaller truck arrived, this one beeping as it backed in, its brakes squealing as it stopped. The driver hopped out with a clipboard for Edith to sign, then opened the rear door.

We all gasped. There, swinging in twelve huge bird cages, were twelve brightly plumed macaws, all screeching at once as the door opened.

"The macaws who are gonna train the llamas," Edith shouted, running to sign for her bird delivery.

The Candelario family poured from their truck and were now scurrying over to help Edith unload the macaws. There were three men and two women, a teenage girl and two young boys.

"It was me or the circus," Edith bragged, nodding at the Candelarios. "I got a bilingual lawyer and made 'em a better deal. They used to be trapeze artists before they got into birds." The Flying Candelarios smiled and nodded their greetings, obviously unable to speak a word of English, but delighted to meet us all.

"What llamas?" Brian said, his eyes almost falling out of his head.

Edith shook her head. "Don't you remember my airport llamas idea?" Edith said. "I figure we can use 'em all over the city. You have never seen such a handy animal to have around. 'Specially for hauling stuff. Really."

"Oh, I heard about them in school," Erica said. "You can make a fortune breeding them."

Edith winked. "That's my Plan B if the airport idea doesn't pan out."

"Llamas?" Brian's voice cracked as he repeated himself. "How many?"

Edith grinned. "Thirty-eight," she said, clicking her tongue to indicate great wisdom. "Now *there's* a smart investment."

Brian and I just stared at each other, our mouths frozen open in matching ovals. Finally Brian croaked, "This must have cost her a million bucks!"

"Oh, perfect—here they come now," Edith said, turning her attention to the street where a gigantic rig was groaning through the gates and bending bushes.

"Yippee!" Bennett yelled, running with his brothers towards the truck. "Let's ride 'em!"

"But how..." Grayson stammered.

"A stroke of genius, Grayson," Edith said. "You can't just let wild llamas loose at the airport, right?"

Grayson shrugged. After living with Edith, he wasn't so sure.

"They have to be trained," Edith said. "Somebody's got to sit out here and tell 'em what to do. Over and over."

Brian was counting under his breath, as all thirty-eight llamas lumbered down the ramp like miniature camels.

"So," Edith went on, "I figure the best person to repeat themselves isn't a person at all. It's a macaw!"

Grayson smiled. He was obviously getting drawn in by Edith's logic.

"I'm going to station a macaw in each of these trees all over the yard," Edith said. "That way, wherever the llamas go, they'll hear instructions about loading luggage."

"What—" Brian shrieked, verging on hysteria— "'The white zone is for loading and unloading only?'"

Edith chuckled. "No," she said, "they'll learn what to do in Spanish. That's where the Candelario family comes in. They're professional bird trainers."

"Wait a minute," I said, not believing my ears. "You brought a family here from Argentina to train the macaws to train the llamas?"

Edith beamed. "I smell another Nobel prize," she crowed. "Hey! Señor Candelario. Ood-fay is in the ouse-hay."

I cringed at Edith's attempts to communicate, and Erica, who had studied Spanish in school, quickly stepped in to help.

"You'd think Pig Latin would cover all Latin languages," I could hear Edith grousing.

"Well," Grayson said, "once the birds are trained, I guess the Candelarios will go home, or to the circus—"

"Or to a mental institution," Brian growled, "*with* the Taylors..."

Grayson smiled. "I think it's a good idea."

Brian stared at his eldest son. "That should elicit alarm of the grandest proportion," Brian said. "I agreed with Edith once and I couldn't eat for two days."

"Brian!" I said.

"She doesn't even have permission to do this!" Brian yelled, his comment lost in the din of squawking birds and squealing children. "Do you think the city will let someone just start up a...a llama union?"

"Well, as she pointed out, there's always Plan B," I said. I stared at Edith and marveled that someone so enraging could also be so engaging. Here was the most infuriating woman in the world, but every one of us loved her to death. In fact, as I glanced at my panic-stricken husband, I realized that death was not completely out of the question.

"And what about the macaws?" Brian said, his voice elevated into a completely different register. "You want to live in a jungle? You think they're not going to wake the dead, screaming in Spanish at four-thirty every morning?"

The Candelarios were now unloading drums of macaw and llama food from their truck, almost creating a stampede as they pried the lid off a drum of food pellets and the llamas got wind of it.

"It's a literal zoo!" Brian shouted, dodging a llama and bumping into one of the wooden cows.

"But if they breed and she really can sell the babies," I said, trying to keep Brian from having a stroke, "it could be a whole sideline."

"What's my business card going to say—" Brian said, veins bulging in his neck—"'Llama Broker'?"

Soon the huge yard teemed with nine leaping children, twenty wooden cows, twelve flapping birds and thirty-eight woolly llamas, chewing grass and glancing regally about their new domain.

"It's worse than the twelve days of Christmas!" Brian said, his voice hoarse from screaming and beads of perspiration covering his forehead.

"Let's sit down," I said, trying to think of a way to calm him short of calling 911.

Brian slumped onto the front steps. "How can this be happening to me?" he mumbled, defeated.

Edith overheard him and joined us on the porch. "Ain't it the greatest?" she bellowed.

"Edith," Brian said, his voice edged with hysteria. "There is no way you are going to get permission to use those llamas at the airport." Then he muttered, "My guardian angel must have a drinking problem."

Edith threw back her head and cackled. "I'm so glad I got you, Brian. If it weren't for you, I'd never have any contagious plans," she said.

"You mean contingency plans?" I asked.

"Exactly," Edith said. "Brian makes me think of all kinds of great back-up ideas. I figure I can always use his llamas to help build the monorail over the dolphin tanks."

Brian opened his mouth to argue about the llamas not being his idea at all, then stopped. "What monorail? What dolphin tanks?"

Edith laughed and whacked Brian happily on the back. "The ones I'm building if your dolphin satellite idea doesn't work out." Then she swung her arms wide, with a twinkle in her eye, and said, "Edith Land."

THE END